Derek Lavelle

VIC

Also by the same author:
'In the Beginning'. An introduction to the Genesis account of creation.
Available from Dunestone Publications, Milber Industrial Estate, Newton Abbot, Devon.

VICTORY IN JESUS

Roger Price

Marshalls

Marshalls Paperbacks
Marshall Morgan & Scott
3 Beggarwood Lane, Basingstoke, Hants RG23 7LP

First published by Marshall Morgan & Scott 1982

Reprinted
Impression number
10 9 8 7 6 5 4 3 2 – 86 85 84 83

All Scriptures are quoted from the New International Version except where indicated.
KJV = KING JAMES VERSION.
NASV = NEW AMERICAN STANDARD VERSION.

ISBN 0 551 01007 X

Photoset by Rowland Phototypesetting Ltd
Bury St Edmunds, Suffolk
Printed in Great Britain by
Hunt Barnard Printing Ltd, Aylesbury, Bucks.

TO MY WIFE

Contents

Foreword

In my ministry to the Body of Christ at home and abroad I have been discovering amongst the Lord's people a wistful longing after the reality of the victorious life in Jesus. It is, therefore, an especial joy to me that Roger Price, whose friendship and fellowship I have treasured for more than a decade, has produced a book which abundantly matches the need, and which should be recommended reading for all who are eager to have a part in God's purposes for our generation.

It is an excellent thing when a man has a profound knowledge and love of the Bible. It is yet more valuable when the same man possesses the rare ability to present the truths of Scripture in such a way that the proverbial 'man in the street' can readily appreciate and enjoy them. I would affirm, however, that the author's achievement in this book transcends both his masterly grasp of the subject and the happy art of imparting knowledge. Under the deceptively simple title *Victory in Jesus* he has made it gloriously possible for his readers to realise in their lives the truth of the victory, and the victory of the truth.

Victory in Jesus – has been the theme of so many sermons, hymns and rousing songs that to-day's Christians may well be forgiven if they assume that they know whatever is to be known about the subject. Nevertheless, to claim a victory presupposes a war, and all too many of the Lord's people have no clear idea that they are enlisted in an army, and still less notion of the nature and capabilities of the enemy. As a whole, we who are members of the Body of Christ have not yet comprehended the position, the privilege and the authority entrusted to us and invested in us by the Head of the Church, our glorious Lord Jesus.

Roger Price has succeeded in revealing the situation as GOD sees it, and as He desires that we should view it with Him. As the chapters unfold, gripping the imagination and firing the heart, we can enter into the revelation of God's perfect plan for the triumphant reign of the Lord and Christ, and the Church triumphantly reigning with Him in life.

When we who belong to the Lord have received into the heart of our experience the majestic verities so unmistakably expressed here, we shall have no excuse for continuing to live 'under the circumstances'. Equally, we shall recognise Satan for the impostor he is, defeated and exposed but treacherous to the last, and determine that we will live in the power of the Holy Ghost and no longer succumb to the wiles of the devil. We shall glory in the fact that Jesus Christ is indeed the Mighty Conqueror, the absolute Master, and revel in our new-found experience of triumphing over evil through Him. It is vital that the Church of God should actively demonstrate His power, His joy and His peace in the world to-day.

My prayer is that the truths so faithfully and exultantly proclaimed here will become reality in the lives of God's children, setting their hearts at liberty and bringing them into the maturity of sonship – the fulness of God's purpose for His people. For you who read this book I pray the hearing of the voice of God, and for the author I solicit your prayers that he may long continue to be 'a messenger of the churches, and the glory of Christ.'

Andrew Jordan

Acknowledgments

The production of a manuscript is a long and often arduous task and I have been blessed to have a team of willing workers who have encouraged and supported me. In its production we have all been conscious of God's sustaining power in full measure and our hearts soar in praise to him.

Malcolm Coulson has championed the cause of simpler English and spent many hours improving the text by making it less verbose and less complicated. It is an unenviable task and I am grateful to him.

Denise Daniel has been fast and accurate in her typing and over many, many hours has been uncomplaining and long-suffering. Unstinting in her efforts, she has been a constant encouragement. I am thankful to the Lord for her and her family, and to Juliet Ryall without whose assistance her task would have been very much more difficult.

Jenny Davis's (neé New) cover and illustrations are excellent and are a credit to her painstaking quest for accuracy.

Proof-reading was undertaken by Brian and Pam Melia, and by my own wife, Rosalyn. To all of them I can only say – Thank you.

Thanks too to the Members of the Chichester Christian Fellowship for their prayers and support.

Introduction

The purpose of this book is to set out the truth concerning the victory which is the right of every person who has received Christ as his saviour. One of the great tragedies of our day is that our enemy the devil is still managing to cause Christians suffering and discouragement through his bluffs and threatenings, because many of them do not know what rights they have in Christ, and those that do are often not stirred up enough to claim them. Satan has used the ignorance of believers to dupe them into accepting defeat without a murmur of protest.

On the one hand 'Our adversary the devil prowls around seeking those whom he may devour' but on the other hand, as God said to the believers of old, 'My people are destroyed from lack of knowledge' (Hosea 4.6). The result of these two things together is that many believers act as a people under seige – cramped, afraid and fearful – instead of realising that through Christ's victory they are 'more than conquerors', 'the head and not the tail', and that the devil has absolutely no rights on any part of their lives.

My prayer is that every one of God's beloved children reading this book will take in and digest the words so that instead of entertaining and occupying them for a few minutes, the revelations stated here may become part of their everyday lives. 'Thy words were found and I did eat them and thy word was unto me the joy and rejoicing of my heart' (Jer. 15.16 KJV).

1: An enemy exposed

'If God exists and is a God of love, how is it that there is so much suffering in the world and why does God permit cruelty and injustice to carry on?' The questioner was an earnest (and sincere) seventeen-year-old who had approached me after a sixth form discussion about Christianity. He was expressing a question which is frequently asked and one with which most Christians are continually confronted. The main fault with the question is that it pre-supposes that God is the only one to be considered when viewing the present world situation, and does not allow for the presence of an evil influence. Most people are highly sceptical about the existence of God himself and so do not easily entertain the idea that some other supernatural personality may have also played a part.

It is clear however that if God had been the only one involved the world around us today would be perfect, just as he is. When he created the earth, the Bible tells us that after every phase 'God saw that it was good.' When dry land appeared; when the plant-life was created and grew; when the sun, moon and stars appeared; when the sea-creatures were placed in the waters and the birds flew in the air, and when the animals were created on the dry land the testimony of Genesis is that it was all good. Indeed after the final act of creation, when man himself was created and all was complete, the word of God says that 'God saw all that He had made and it was *very* good' (Gen. 1.31).

However, when we look around at the creation today with its disease, poverty, bereavement, disaster, war, accident and the sheer wickedness of one man to another, we are obliged to ask; how has this come about?

In the thirteenth chapter of the Gospel of Matthew Jesus tells the parable of a man who planted good seed in his field, but who found weeds or tares growing with the wheat at the end of the harvest. When his servant asked him how this had happened his reply was 'An enemy did this' (Matt. 13.28). It isn't that the owner had done anything wrong or that the original seed was polluted; the problem had arisen through someone else's activity.

When I was an atheist I would often taunt Christians by saying that if God did exist, then from all the evidence I could see in the world today he must be a very evil being indeed, and certainly not the God of love they claimed. How could it be otherwise with all the suffering around us? I was trying to get a response from Christians which would force them into mentioning the devil. Once he came up the argument was won, I thought, for surely anyone who had to resort to such unscientific, old-fashioned mumbo-jumbo was scarcely fit to be taken seriously.

Actually it was I who was being foolish, for I had been taken in by one of the devil's cleverest ploys. He is an enemy whose best defence is to go unrecognised, and so unchallenged, for a world which denies his existence is a world in which he can work unhindered. His strategy is infinitely more cunning than that of Quislings or guerillas. He is the author of the devastation we see around us and the one who masterminded the present evil, yet is so carefully hidden that only a small proportion of our society will even admit that he exists. The devil has been very subtle. He has inspired a portrait of himself which creates disbelief. While the Bible declares him to be the embodiment of all that is beautiful, even appearing as an angel of light (2 Cor.11.14), he has put around the idea that he is a creature with red skin, slit green eyes, horns and a forked tail, a picture so laughable that only the simple-minded or insane would take it seriously. The devil doesn't mind such an unflattering portrait when it serves his purpose.

It is one of many ways in which the tracks to his true identity have been covered over. Ezekiel 28.14 describes him as a *cherub* – the name given to one of the angelic orders. The cherubs are the highest-ranking angels, glamorous and beautiful creatures. Yet Satan has inspired a picture of them which is totally unreal and today cherubs are visualized as rather plump babies with pink cheeks, bows and arrows and carefully placed ribbons. Hardly a stately home in England is without them. The result is that most people are fooled into believing that his existence is best relegated to the realms of superstition which, though acceptable in more primitive times, has no place in this age of science and enlightenment. Modern man prides himself on his sophistication and yet as Romans 1.22 says, 'professing themselves to be wise, they became fools' (KJV).

Nothing is more dangerous than an undetected, unlocated foe. Thankfully for us 'The Word of the Lord stands forever' (1 Peter 1.25) and in the sacred pages of scripture the enemy is clearly exposed and revealed in all his wickedness. We must face up to the fact that he *does* exist and is still active in his rebellion against God.

This book, however, concerns the victory which Jesus wrought over the devil and explores the rights which are ours because we are believers. In Ephesians 4.27 we are told 'do not give the devil a foothold'. With such a subtle enemy this can only be obeyed by knowing who he is and how he operates, by knowing where we stand now that we are in Christ and by being diligent in our daily walk. 'Be self-controlled and alert. Your enemy the devil prowls around like a roaring lion looking for someone to devour. Resist him, standing firm in the faith. . . .' (1 Peter 5.8 and 9).

With the Bible so freely available to us no member of the

Church of Jesus Christ should be robbed through lack of knowledge. The Bible is the only source to which we can turn to find out about this arch-fiend and so it is in its pages we must look to see him revealed. The career of the devil is revealed in detail in two particular passages of the Old Testament: in Ezekiel 28 and Isaiah 14.

In Ezekiel 28.1–10 there is a description of the ruler of Tyre or, as the King James Version of the Bible calls him, 'the prince of Tyre'. He was a man called Ittobaal the Second, and his riches and obvious talents had increased his pride to the point where he had taken full credit for the wealth and commercial standing of Tyre and now claimed that he was divine. God prophesied that He would bring invaders into Tyre who would destroy his dreams and eventually put him to death.

Directly after this passage comes a mysterious counterpart in verses 11–19 which is addressed to another character called 'the king of Tyre'. The superhuman descriptions in this passage make it likely that this is a description of the real power behind the throne – the devil himself. Here, typically, the devil had hidden himself allowing the ruler and his people to think that Ittobaal was the real power and it is only the word of the Lord through Ezekiel which reveals the true position. In verses 11–15 we see the career of the devil before his rebellion against God and a description of his beauty, and in verses 16–19 God's judgment upon him is prophesied.

'The word of the Lord came to me: "Son of man, take up a lament concerning the king of Tyre and say to him: 'This is what the Sovereign Lord says:

> "You were the model of perfection, full of wisdom and perfect in beauty. You were in Eden, the garden of God; every precious stone adorned you: ruby, topaz and emerald, crysolite, onyx and jasper, sapphire, turquoise and beryl.
>
> Your settings and mountings were made of gold; on the

day you were created they were prepared.
You were anointed as a guardian cherub, for so I ordained you.
You were on the holy mount of God;
You walked among the fiery stones.
You were blameless in your ways from the day you were created till wickedness was found in you."' (v11–15)

This passage refers to the one whose names include 'Lucifer' and 'the Son of the morning' (Isaiah 14.12. KJV). Those names show how stunningly beautiful he was, for 'Lucifer' means 'bringer of light' or 'the shining or glamorous one' and in this passage of Ezekiel some of his beauty is clearly described. He is still a most attractive, startling and intelligent being.

Ezekiel expresses it by saying that Lucifer was 'the model of perfection, full of wisdom and perfect in beauty', rather than the monster most imagine. When he was created God adorned him with beauty. But notice that as a created being he does not have the attributes of God.

1: He isn't omnipresent (everywhere at once) but can only be in one place at a time. His influence is widely spread through his demonic agents but this does not compare with the omnipresence of God.

2. He is not omniscient (all-knowing) – he knows much more than we do, but nothing like the total that God knows. Again, it is his fallen angels who provide him with information and while limited themselves (1 Peter 1.12), they have a 'spy-network' around the whole universe.

3. Similarly he is not omnipotent (all-powerful) – he is certainly powerful but has nothing to compare with God's infinite power. Many believers talk about the devil as if he were God's equal and in doing so they inadvertently glorify him beyond what is true. While we must never mock or be foolishly flippant about him, we must always think and act in true biblical perspective and not be taken in by his false claims.

When first created God appointed him to the highest office – he was 'a guardian cherub' who guarded the very throne-room of God. As Lucifer walked among the fiery stones he was a crown of praise to God, a being who reflected the creative power of the Master, 'till iniquity was found in thee' (Ez.28.15) (KJV). The day came when his abundance of beauty and talents turned his head and pride became his downfall, and he turned from serving God. No wonder Ittobaal the Second had been such a willing partner, for in him the devil had found a kindred spirit.

Ezekiel 28.16–19 tells of the devil's fall and speaks of the judgment upon him:

'Through your widespread trade you were filled with violence, and you sinned. So I drove you in disgrace from the mount of God, and I expelled you, O guardian cherub, from among the fiery stones.
Your heart became proud on account of your beauty, and you corrupted your wisdom because of your splendour. . . .' (v16 and 17)

'Your widespread trade' is a Hebrew idiom for 'prosperity' and refers to the talents and outstanding beauty which God had invested in him.

To trace the growth of the devil's pride we have to turn to the second passage, Isaiah 14.12–15. Again the reference comes in a passage addressed to a ruler – the king of Babylon. Half-way through, the real power behind the throne is revealed:

'How you have fallen from heaven, O morning star, son of the dawn! You have been cast down to the earth, you who once laid low the nations! You said in your heart, 'I will ascend to heaven;
I will raise my throne above the stars of God;
I will sit enthroned on the mount of assembly, on
the utmost heights of the sacred mountain.
I will ascend above the tops of the clouds;

I will make myself like the Most High"[1] (v12–14)

The King James Version of the Bible translates v12 as 'How art thou fallen from heaven, O Lucifer, son of the morning!' The fact that he can still appear as an angel of light shows that his beauty is largely undiminished. So many have been deceived by the devil simply because when he has appeared to them his beauty has contrasted with their awful preconceived picture of him. With the Bible as our reference we should not be so deceived.

The fall of Satan is outlined by five phrases all beginning with 'I will', which reminds us that sin begins in our free-will and is progressive. At first his desire was to live as God did, permanently in the heavenly throne-room. Then he plotted to raise his throne above the stars of God (v13) – a reference to the other angels. Not content with the fact that God had appointed him to a superior rank, he wanted to rise still further and to accomplish it by his own efforts.

It was only a matter of time before the rebellion was complete. The third 'I will' expresses his desire to extend his rule, so that not only angelic beings are under his control but the whole of the earth as well. 'I will ascend above the tops of the clouds' (v14) suggests a desire to replace God as sovereign of the universe. Out of some 150 references to 'clouds' in the Bible over 100 are connected with the presence of God – God 'makes the clouds his chariot' (Psalm 104.3) and is said to ride on them (Isaiah 19.1 and Matt.24.30). When the presence of God filled the Temple of Solomon it was seen as a cloud – I Kings 8.10.

Finally 'I will make myself like the Most High' (v14) expresses the extent of the devil's power madness. He desires to have the essence, attributes and character of God himself. As we have seen, he can never achieve this, but one of his lies is to convince people that he already has.

With Satan expelled from his place in the throne-room of God, the earth became the arena for his revolt. The scarred earth we see before us reflects that battle. Whether believers like it or not, and most do not, we are inevitably involved in this deadly war. Some Christians mistakenly believe that if they ignore it, or take a neutral stance, then peace will follow. Such reactions can only please the devil and hinder the purposes of God. Whether we mistakenly believe that we can live at peace with the devil or not, he knows that he can never live at peace with us. An attempt to be neutral is to side with the devil. A driver in a car has three choices – to go forward towards his destination, to reverse away from his destination or to stay in neutral. The first choice alone will achieve his objective; the other two have the same effect, which is to fail to reach his destination.

A believer 'in neutral' is no worry for the devil and as such frees him to devote more energy to other areas of the battle. A neutral out-of-fellowship, passive believer, while still saved by grace, is in effect and in terms of this battle an enemy of Christ. This is why in the New Testament we are constantly encouraged to 'stand firm'; 'gird up your loins'; 'be strong in the Lord'.

'Therefore, my dear brothers, stand firm. Let nothing move you. Always give yourselves fully to the work of the Lord, because you know that your labour in the Lord is not in vain' (1 Cor.15.58).

'Therefore, prepare your minds for action; be self-controlled, set your hope fully on the grace to be given you when Jesus Christ is revealed' (1 Peter 1.13).

'Finally, be strong in the Lord and in his mighty power. Put on the full armour of God so that you can take your stand against the devil's schemes' (Eph.6.10 and 11).

The word of God spells out the strategy which the devil adopts in this battle. That is why Paul, writing in 2 Corinthians 2.11, declares that 'we are not unaware of his schemes'. If believers allow the devil openings he will make full use of them.

Our enemy is identified by several names and titles. He

is called Abaddon (Rev.9.11); 'the accuser of the brethren' (Rev.12.10) KJV; 'that ancient serpent' (Rev.12.9); Apollyon (Rev.9.11); Beelzebub (Mark 3.22); Belial (2 Cor.6.15); 'the one which deceives the whole world' (Rev.12.9); 'the devil' (Matt.4.1); 'the dragon' (Rev.12.9); 'the evil one' (John 17.15 and 1 John 5.18); 'the father of lies' (John 8.44); 'the god of this world' (2 Cor.4.4) KJV; 'a liar' (John 8.44); 'a murderer' (John 8.44); 'the prince of demons' (Mark 3.22); 'the prince of the power of the air' (Eph.2.2) KJV; 'the prince of this world' (John 12.31); 'Satan' (Matt.4.10) and 'the tempter' (1 Thess. 3.5).

These names are revealing and should be studied carefully. The title 'prince of the power of the air', for example, is one which reveals his influence over the face of the earth. The Bible shows that an evil angelic council seeks to control the affairs of the earth and it has appointed angelic agents who try to control the affairs of each nation. One such angel, called the prince of the kingdom of Persia, appears in Daniel 10, where he succeeded in stopping an angel of God from communicating with Daniel for twenty-one days. It was only when reinforcements arrived from heaven in the form of the archangel Michael that the task could be completed. Every nation has such angels over them which are called 'powers of this dark world' or 'the spiritual forces of evil in the heavenly realms' (Ephesians 6.12). The overall council which directs them is called 'the power of the air' (Eph.2.2). Satan is the prince of this controlling body. Politicians and others may work hard to change things, but the only real lasting change will come if the work of this angelic hierarchy is thwarted. A heavenly, spiritual people are the only ones who can do it and of these there will be much to say in later chapters.

The name 'devil' is the Greek word 'diabolos' which comes from 'diaballo' which means 'to divide'; 'to set at variance'; 'to accuse'; 'to slander'; 'to reject'; 'misrepresent' or 'deceive'. Hence the word 'devil' is usually translated as 'slanderer'. So often when we find ourselves experiencing division, accusation, or deception we tend to think that our problem is a carnal one – one person against another, or one group against another. But with an enemy like the devil it is time we took more notice of his characteristic spiritual activity.

'Satan' is from the Hebrew word '*shatan*' which means 'to lie in wait'; 'to oppose'; 'to be hostile to' and from that has come the meaning 'adversary' or 'opponent'. The constant cry from hell against the work of God is 'let the work cease' and anything which hinders the progress of the saints of God is employed.

Both 'Abaddon' and 'Apollyon' mean 'the destroyer'. Satan's power lust is so great that everyone, if necessary, will be destroyed to achieve his aim. Human suffering is meaningless to him against his desire for full control. All the sin and misery of our world past, present and future, and all the misery of hell is the result of his agency and influence.

From these things we can now outline the main activities of Satan. First we will deal with his main strategy in the lives of unbelievers.

To nonbelievers Satan is 'the god of this world' and most men and women are his unwitting disciples. They live lives of devotion to his ways and ideas even though they would deny his existence. It is rare for one of his followers to depart or revolt. His way is easy, his path is broad – indeed the world would call it 'doing what comes naturally'. God, however, calls it sin and falling short of his glory.

Satan's main aim is to leave the nonbeliever undisturbed in the way that leads to destruction. He works to keep him in spiritual blindness and to snatch away any seed of truth that is planted. He doesn't know who will be saved and who won't and so attempts to stop the light of the glorious gospel of Jesus Christ from taking root wherever it is placed. In Luke 8 Jesus tells the parable of the sower and in the interpretation says 'The seed is the Word of God. Those along the path are the ones who hear, and then the devil comes and takes away the word from their hearts, so that they cannot believe and be saved' (Luke 8.11 and 12). Satan and his legions are constantly working at this. As long as men are unregenerate they are his allies and he does not want to lose them from his kingdom.

'The god of this age has blinded the minds of unbelievers, so that they cannot see the light of the gospel of the glory of Christ' (2 Cor. 4.4).

It is not only a negative campaign but a positive one too. Satan is active in the miraculous. When Moses went to Pharaoh and threw down his staff and turned it into a snake, Pharaoh simply summoned the wise men and sorcerers of his own land and they repeated it (Ex. 7.8–13). Many nonbelievers today are very impressed by the miraculous and are not worried about the source of the power – indeed it doesn't seem to matter what power made a miracle occur, or healed a person, as long as there is a sign or the person is well again. The waiting lists for spiritualists, faith-healers and astrologers get ever longer, and once their victims are impressed the trap is sprung. A prophetic passage in 2 Thessalonians 2 actually says this will happen on an increasing scale: 'The coming of the lawless one will be in accordance with the work of Satan displayed in all kinds of counterfeit miracles, signs and wonders, and in every sort of evil that deceives those who are perishing' (v9 and 10).

As far as Satan's power is concerned, the nonbeliever's appetite seems limitless – but introduce God's power and often the reaction is different. Recently a non-Christian relative and her family came to stay with our family. She had read with great interest accounts of the healing which had occurred bv Satan's power and which were reported in certain Sunday newspapers. While staying with us her eight-year-old son became ill, looking very pale and crying in pain. As he was in our house we decided to pray for him and claim healing and release. After prayer I told the mother that within half-an-hour he would be fine.

When twenty minutes later he walked in for lunch radiant, free from pain and with a healthy colour, her mouth dropped open in amazement. But within a few seconds she had recovered her composure and dismissed the whole thing. Any seed of belief had been successfully retrieved by the devil's troops. Satan's miraculous hemlock, however, is left to take root and grow.

Satan does this on a grand scale and in Revelation 12.9 and 20.3 and 8 he is seen as the deceiver of the nations. He it is who has propagated false ideas and concepts, the 'things taught by demons' (1 Timothy 4.1). Evolution, humanism, communism and many other doctrines are part of his evil scheme in so far as they induce in people's minds denial of the existence of God.[1]

Of more concern to us is Satan's strategy towards believers. The following is a list of the main ways in which Satan tries to render believers inoperative.

1. He accuses them. (Job.1.6–11; Zechariah 3.1 and 2; Rev.12.9 and 10). So many believers are under condemnation all the time and as a result live defeated lives, often afraid to trust themselves.

2. He tries to keep believers away from God's word so that they will not be those of whom Jesus said 'ye shall know the truth and the truth shall make you free' (John 8.32 KJV).

3. He causes tiredness and drowsiness especially at prayer-times, in Bible studies and in times of spiritual activity.

4. He attacks believers by directing their eyes away from the Lord and onto:-

self (1 Corinthians 1.10–12);

others (1 Kings 19.1–3);
and possessions (Hebrews 13.5 and 6).

5. He frightens believers especially with regard to death (Heb. 2.14 and 15).
6. He causes believers to worry (1 Peter 5.7–9). Worry is unbelief because it is based on the assumption that God doesn't care or that he can't help.
7. He attempts to cause believers to become more occupied with other things which will stop them being so fervent and dedicated in the work of the Lord. These attacks do not only include temptations to sin which will draw the believer out of fellowship with God but are often far more subtle. Careers or very good humane causes can be used to preoccupy the believer.
8. Satan attempts to get the believer in the wrong place (1 Thess. 2.18); doing the wrong things (Galatians 5.7) or thinking and believing wrong doctrine (1 Timothy 4.1 and Eph. 4.14). Part of this is the devil's attempt to get believers preoccupied with him rather than with the Lord.

Many of these will be covered when the rights of believers are examined in later chapters. The victory that Christ has given to us who believe is so great that we need never be taken in by these things or subject to them.

To know who the devil is and how he works is to remove his cover, and when he is exposed much of his effectiveness is gone.

We must next concern ourselves with what are undoubtedly the most prominent events in Satan's career. The first of these is his meeting with and triumph over the first Adam in the Garden of Eden; and the second, which will preoccupy us for most of this book, is Satan's encounter with the Last Adam, Jesus Christ. This latter encounter resulted in defeat and humiliation from which he will never recover, and sealed his fate for all eternity. As John testifies in 1 John 3.8 'The reason the Son of God appeared was to destroy the devil's work'.

2: The spiral of defeat

Before we go onto to examine the victory which is ours in Christ, we must look at another source of defeat for the believer. In the preface of his book 'The Screwtape Letters', C. S. Lewis makes a very important statement. 'There are,' he says 'two equal and opposite errors into which our race can fall about devils. One is to disbelieve in their existence. The other is to believe and feel an excessive, unhealthy interest in them'.[1]

I often receive phone-calls and visits from people who claim that the devil or one of his demons is attacking them, or that they need deliverance. Sometimes they are right, but often they are blaming the devil for something which has nothing to do with him. The devil would be very rich indeed if he received damages for all the false and slanderous statements made about him. Often the trouble has its source not in him but in us. The devil *is* evil and has masterminded the present world turmoil, but one of the factors that has allowed him to have such influence is man's sinfulness. The problems of some people can't be cured by deliverance, but only by the application of the Cross of Christ to their lives and putting off of the old self (Eph.4.22).

The fact of man's sinfulness and its' root, the fall of mankind, is central to the Christian faith for it is the reason why men need a saviour. Indeed the Bible is clear that human nature is totally depraved and that this fallen nature has been transmitted to the entire human race with the exception of the man Jesus Christ e.g. Romans 5.12,15 and 17.

A world which rejects the need for a saviour must, of course, also reject the doctrine of the fall of man. Many of the beliefs and creeds so popularly embraced by the world assume inherent goodness in man; that man is 'an angel in the making' and is improving. Evil is explained in various ways. Some say that man has not had sufficient time to develop fully and that in due course he will learn by experience how to handle himself; others say that the problem is one of environment so that the answer to evil is to correct the conditions in which men are brought up. Still others say that evil is a problem of education – that if we show someone what is best they will adopt it. All of them agree about one thing; that man's problem is due to something lacking[2] – time, proper environment or knowledge. The concept of sin, they say, is old-fashioned and the quicker it is dropped the better.

Most people with young children, however, will know that in fact what causes bad behaviour isn't something lacking, but something that is only too present – a fallen nature. A baby or young child never has to be taught how to be bad, but always how to be good. I have never yet heard a mother teaching her son how to lose his temper, or cry until he gets what he wants. That comes naturally. An elderly woman who had worked among the poor in the East End of London during the first world war said recently on the radio that she had believed in those days that if only people would get enough to eat, a higher standard of housing and entertainment, all crime and vandalism would stop. Yet, she continued, though conditions today are incomparably better, crime and vandalism are more rampant. Her philosophy was bankrupt to explain it. The tragedy for her and us is that the fallen nature is positively, actively and effectively *there*. Evil isn't 'all-in-your-head', as the founder of the Christian Scientists, Mary Baker Eddy would tell us; it isn't 'an illusion'.[3] It is only too real and the trouble with man is that he is possessed by a positive tendency towards wickedness. Only the Bible outlines how this sinful tendency entered human history.

Genesis reveals that man was the crown and climax of all God's work. How poor the evolutionary scheme makes man in comparison with the nobility attributed to him by Scripture. Compare the following quotation from the writings of Jacques Monod, who views man's creation as a fortunate but fantastically improbable chance, with the account in Genesis 1.26–28. 'The universe was not pregnant with life nor the biosphere with man. Our number just came up in a Monte Carlo game. Is it any wonder if, like the person who has just made a million at the casino, we feel strange and a little unreal.'[4]

'Then God said, "Let us make man in our image, in our likeness, and let them rule over the fish of the sea and the birds of the air, over the livestock, over all the earth, and over all the creatures that move along the ground".

So God created man in his own image, in the image of God he created him; male and female he created them.

God blessed them and said to them, "Be fruitful and increase in number; fill the earth and subdue it. Rule over the fish of the sea and the birds of the air and over every living creature that moves on the ground".'

It is the belief that man is not an animal but bears the very image of God which has been a source of dignity and inspiration through human history. Here is the basic reason why our law gives the same rights to rich and poor, strong and weak, intelligent and stupid, so that the drunk in the gutter has as many rights in law as the richest, most successful businessman. Irrespective of his or her present condition each person is made in God's image and is therefore of inestimable value.

In Genesis 2 we see the original and eternal purpose of God for man – he was to rule over the earth. Incidentally, this is not a different account of creation, but simply fills in the details not covered in the overall picture given in Genesis 1. All fish, birds, animals and the earth itself were to be his realm, and man, the pinnacle of all that God had created, was to be king.

'Fill . . . subdue . . . rule' were the commands that God delivered to Adam. Even the command 'to be fruitful and increase in number' was not given just to crowd the earth with people but that the children produced would be trained in their rightful 'dominion', and so extend the area of that domain until the planet was covered. Filling it alone was not enough – rulership and dominion were the real tasks. Genesis 2.8 is also worded very carefully 'Now the Lord God had planted a garden in the east, in Eden; and there he put the man he had formed'. The Garden of Eden did not cover the whole earth as some mistakenly believe, but was an area small enough for Adam and Eve to manage. In this area Adam and Eve were to bring up and train their family, work and harvest the land for food. 'The Lord God took the man and put him in the Garden of Eden to work it and take care of it' (v15).

By the account given in Scripture it was a magnificent paradise. Many have tried to find it but the extensive changes which were caused by the world-wide catastrophe known as Noah's flood make such a search futile. Even though the Tigris and Euphrates are the last of the four rivers mentioned in Genesis 2.10–14 the geographical changes which occurred in the flood make it highly doubtful whether they can be identified as those which flow today. In this paradise seed-bearing plants (Genesis 1.29) and trees (Genesis 2.9) grew in abundance, and life was rich and fulfilled.

Sinless Adam lived as king in an unfallen and fruitful world. Two tests awaited him, however, and both were directed towards the area of his free-will. First he had positively to obey God's commands and thereby show that he was choosing to love God; and secondly he had to resist the attacks of the tempter. Both of these tests were the reason for the presence of the tree called 'tree of the knowledge of good and evil' in the Garden (Genesis 2.9). Adam could do and have whatever he wanted except that he was not to eat from this tree. There was nothing wrong in the tree itself; it was simply the thing which would show Adam's loyalty. He would have to choose for God or for the devil. To choose for God meant obeying him and saying 'no' to the devil; choosing for the devil meant abandoning God's command and actively obeying the devil's words. The waging of this battle was done according to God's justice.

Samuel Limbach expresses it well: 'Satan is prince of this world. Faced by him man was to represent God's justice on earth. He was to rule over creation in the name of God and to work God's works within it. Thus the enemy would be driven back legally. But if the liberation of the world was to be effected wholly according to justice and righteousness, then an opportunity had to be given Satan, God's foe, to extend his world rule of evil over man as well as being permitted to tempt him.'[5]

Genesis 3.1–5 records the outcome. Here the devil comes in the form of one of the animals in the garden and he directs his initial attack against Eve. He first of all asks Eve whether God has said 'You must not eat from any tree in the garden'. Eve repeats the words that God had said to Adam and ends with the warning he had given 'you will die' (v3).

Satan uses this to present his own doctrine to Eve in contradiction to the word of God. ' "You will not surely die" the serpent said to the woman. "For God knows that when you eat of it your eyes will be opened, and you will be like God, knowing good and evil." ' (v4 & 5). This is a very cunning attack and one which Satan still employs. He says that God is jealously guarding his own postion and is not willing to share what should be available to all. His insinuation is that God is a 'spoil-sport', a 'kill-joy' who is only happy when people are miserable. This same thought is whispered into the ears of the young today as demons lie about the joys of illicit sex and drugs. 'God doesn't want to see you liberated, enjoying yourself, living life with a capital "L"'. The misery and death which are the result of these activities and God's desire to spare people from these are concealed.

Eve was taken in completely by Satan's words and began a process which has resulted in all that besets us in the present world: 'When the woman saw that the fruit of the tree was good for food and pleasing to the eye, and also desirable for gaining wisdom, she took some and ate it. She also gave some to her husband who was with her and he ate it' (Genesis 3.6).

It is interesting to note that while the New Testament declares that Eve was deceived (1 Timothy 2.14) it always refers to this act of disobedience as Adam's sin. Why is this? The reason is that there was no deception in Adam's act. It is likely that the moment Eve's lips touched the fruit something physical occurred which showed Adam clearly what the results of his disobedience would be. Perhaps he and Eve were clothed with light as God Himself is described in Psalm 104.2. The resurrection body which all believers receive at the resurrection certainly shines as did the glorious body of Jesus on the Mount of Transfiguration, and it may be that this is a full restoration of the human body as it was before the fall. If their bodies did shine, then clearly Eve's body would have lost its mantle of light the moment disobedience occurred, and Adam would know exactly what he was doing. He chose to do the devil's bidding and to ignore the commandment and warning of God.

His act was the cause of his sin and of the curse which came upon the whole world. He had gone the way of the serpent. Satan was created 'perfect' (Ezekiel 28.15) but later rebelled. Adam was created 'very good' (Genesis 1.31) and now he, too, had rebelled. Neither was forced to rebel and, therefore, each is held accountable for his acts.

God had warned that if Adam and Eve sinned they would die. This raises the question 'why was this penalty not carried out?' The answer is that immediately the act of rebellion occurred, spiritual death, which is separation from God, ensued. It is this spiritual death which opens man to physical death.

Adam and Eve need not have died, but their disobedience robbed them of their immortality. Created immortal, they now become mortal.

Once the fall had occurred the effects were immediate and progressive. Adam's fallen nature was contrary to God and prone to evil. No other human being but Adam became a sinner by sinning – all the rest of us were born sinners, as David says in Psalm 51.5: 'Surely I have been a sinner from birth, sinful from the time my mother conceived me'. Because Adam was the ancestor of mankind and its representative, death established itself upon all his descendants as well (Romans 5.12–21). By this one sinful act Adam came under the domination of Satan, and with the king enslaved, the whole of his realm became the territory of Satan.

The immediate physical effect was that Adam and Eve discovered that they were naked, and experienced a need to conceal that nakedness: 'Then the eyes of both of them were opened, and they realised that they were naked; so they sewed fig leaves together and made coverings for themselves' (Genesis 3.7). Then came the awareness of shame before God: 'Then the man and his wife heard the sound of the Lord God as he was walking in the garden in the cool of the day, and they hid from the Lord God among the trees of the garden' (Genesis 3.8). Fear had replaced the trust and free communion which had previously prevailed and now instead of running to him they ran away.

Relationship with God became difficult and no longer flowed naturally as before.

The Lord then had no option but to remove them from the Garden of Eden, for growing in the garden with the tree of the knowledge of good and evil was another tree called 'the tree of life' (Genesis 2.9). If, in their fallen state, they had been able to gain access to this tree then their bodies, which had immediately begun to experience physical degeneration, could have been healed and immortality regained, but the result would have been a physical immortality sustaining a fallen spirit!

Eric Sauer expresses it well: 'To abide further in Paradise with a continuous renewing of his outward life-power would have meant nothing less for man than the eternal perpetuation of his sin, his condemnation to an unredeemable condition and so to a never-ending destruction. The sinner's bodily deathlessness would be eternal death to his soul and Paradise would have become Hell'.[6]

'And the Lord God said, "The man has now become like one of us, knowing good and evil. He must not be allowed to reach out his hand and take also from the tree of life and eat, and live forever." So the Lord God banished him from the Garden of Eden' (Genesis 3.22 and 23).

So the fall affected Adam both spiritually and physically and these effects were passed on to all his descendants. But there was a further shock to come. Because Adam had rebelled against his Lord, the earth was now permitted to rebel against its lord too. Man, still occupying the position of the lord over the created realm, began to find that realm resisting his ministrations. No more would the ground willingly yield its harvest to Adam. Now he'd have to work for it, and work hard.

> 'Cursed is the ground because of you; through painful toil you will eat of it all the days of your life.
> It will produce thorns and thistles for you
> and you will eat the plants of the field.

By the sweat of your brow you will eat your food
until you return to the ground, since from it you were taken;
for dust you are and to dust you will return' (Genesis 3.17 and 18).

In addition to this, man's body also became his enemy. Just as the ground under man's feet was cursed, so also his physical frame, which was made from the dust of the ground, became subject to physical illness and decay and now actually resisted his spiritual growth.

The corrupt spirit initially rebels against God and resists spiritual understanding, and without a regenerating miracle it does not function as it was designed. But even when this miracle occurs the flesh still battles against the spirit and constantly tends to drag it down.

No area of man's life has remained unaffected and throughout human experience the tendency has always been downwards and away from God. Only the Bible gives a satisfactory explanation of the continuous pattern of decline in human history.

The spiral of defeat which followed the fall is easy to trace in scripture. Genesis 4 begins with the birth of two brothers, Cain and Abel, the first of Adam and Eve's many children (Genesis 5.4). Cain grew to be a farmer as his father was before him, and Abel kept sheep. At this time there was a strict vegetarian diet (Genesis 1.29 and 30) and so it is clear that the sheep were not kept for meat. They were kept for wool to make clothing, for milk and for sacrifice to the Lord. The wool probably testifies to a worsening climate in the earth subsequent to the fall.

The story of Cain and Abel has been recounted by many[7] and it is sufficient for us to note here that due to Cain's jealousy, he rose up and murdered his brother Abel. In Genesis 4.8 we are not told more than that 'Cain attacked his brother Abel and killed him', but when the incident is recalled in 1 John 3.12 we learn much more.

'Do not be like Cain, who belonged to the evil one and murdered his brother. And why did he murder him? Because his own actions were evil and his brother's were righteous.'

The Greek word for 'murder' here is '*sphazo*', and it is a word meaning sacrificial killing. It suggests here that the only killing Cain had seen was that which occurred when a lamb was taken and ceremonially had its throat cut as an offering to the Lord. The use of this Greek word shows us that Cain cut the throat of Abel. Today killing has become commonplace but the shock of this first murder perhaps more than anything else would have demonstrated to Adam and Eve the effect of what they had done. The decline was gathering momentum.

In Genesis 4 we also see the beginning of human society. Within a few generations of the fall man's creative genius was emerging and in his society there was division of labour including the manufacture and use of musical instruments (v21); and bronze and iron tool-making (v22). Yet it was accompanied by the poisonous effects of the fall. The boast of Cain's descendant Lamech, who was the seventh generation from Adam, shows that the decline had continued.

'"Adah and Zillah, listen to me; wives of Lamech, hear my words, I have killed a man for wounding me, a young man for injuring me. If Cain is avenged seven times, then Lamech seventy-seven times"' (Genesis 4.23 and 24).

As the population grew so did the evil until, as we are told in Genesis 6, the Lord looked down on the earth and saw almost uncontrolled wickedness. 'The Lord saw how great man's wickedness on the earth had become, and that every inclination of the thoughts of his heart was only evil all the time' (Genesis 6.5). Noah's Flood was sent because the sin was so great that God could no longer ignore it.

'Now the earth was corrupt in God's sight and was full of violence. God saw how corrupt the earth had become, for all the people on the earth had corrupted their ways. So God said to Noah, 'I am going to put an end to all people, for the earth is filled with violence because of them. I am surely going to destroy both them and the earth (Genesis 6.11–13).

The paradise with which the earth had begun had vanished like a dream and mans' moral descent was accelerating. The instrument which God chose to stem this tide of evil was a world-wide flood which saw the end of the Garden of Eden and changed the earth's surface. After the flood the climate and landscape were immeasurably poorer[8] but the eight people who had survived it (Noah and his family) had the opportunity of a new beginning.

Unfortunately, the society on the earth today, which has descended directly from Noah and his family, shows that while the decline has not been as rapid as before the flood, it has nevertheless been as relentless and all-embracing. Today the earth again is filled with corruption, wickedness and violence and it can only be a matter of time before God intervenes once more – not with water this time, but with fire (2 Peter 3.3–10).

After the flood God repeated to Noah the words he had first spoken to Adam, that he and his descendants were to 'be fruitful and increase in number and fill the earth' (Genesis 9.1). With the exception that now people could eat meat (Genesis 9.3), the calling and instructions were identical, but so unfortunately was the inner corruption which had entered human history at the fall. Increasing technological genius and an increasing appetite for wickedness both typified the new society.

One last illustration, taken from the post-flood civilisation, will serve to demonstrate the continuing downward spiral and the reality of the fall. About 2000 BC the spiritual decline on the earth was so bad that all mankind was again in danger. Godly men (of Melchizedek's stature) were dying without successors and the godly witnesses were very few. It was time for God to intervene. His intervention came with the call of Abraham. 'The God of Glory appeared to our father Abraham while he was still in Mesopotamia, before he lived in Haran. "Leave your country and your people", God said, "and go to the land I will show you"' (Acts 7.2 and 3). He chose a descendant of Shem to be the father of a nation which would be his witness and custodians of his revelation, 'entrusted with the very words of God' (Romans 3.2). Through them God wanted to bless the whole world.

But even with Abraham's descendants the faith and godliness of each successive generation became weaker. Abraham recognised the need for family unity and did as much as he could to maintain it, even allowing his nephew Lot to take advantage of him (Genesis 13). He separated himself from the Canaanite culture, insisting that his son Isaac married a non-Canaanite (Genesis 24) and he built altars and openly worshipped the Lord.

The history of his family reveals that his descendants were not so godly. Family discord grew – Joseph was nearly killed by his brothers (Genesis 37); Onan refused to help his sister-in-law (Genesis 38.8–10); and Judah deceitfully withheld his son from Tamar, his daughter-in-law (Genesis 38.11–15). Relationships with the Canaanites became commonplace – Judah, for example, saw nothing wrong in having sexual relations with a Canaanite sacred prostitute (Genesis 38.15–21). And by Judah's generation no mention is made at all of public worship or testimony. Is it any wonder that by the fourth generation they were enslaved in Egypt?[9]

The Bible shows then that Man, through Adam's sin, is enslaved by the devil and subject to bondage. But this depressing scenario is fortunately not the end of the story. As Paul so aptly says of his own fallen condition, 'what a wretched man I am! Who will rescue me from his body of death?'. But he then goes on to answer the question.

'Thanks be to God – through Jesus Christ our Lord'. (Romans 7.24 and 25).

From this point on we will be examining the Good News which has come through the Lord Jesus Christ.

3: The seed of promise

The scene of defeat which we have just surveyed is the plight of man in rebellion against God – a picture of failure, decline and frustration which, without God's intervention, would have been the inevitable life-long experience of us all.

The consequences of the fall in the life of man are nowhere better examined than in the book of Ecclesiastes. Although its author, Solomon, was a believer he spent most of his later life out of fellowship with God living a life of complete self-indulgence. He wrote the book as an older and wiser man – a man who knew that without God all of man's attempts to gain satisfaction end in desperation and unfulfilment. Certainly in worldly terms he was an impressive figure – the descriptions given of him in the Bible show that very few in history have been his equal. He was handsome, strong, intelligent, skilled, versatile, gifted musically, a botanist and biologist of great standing and fabulously rich. If anyone could have been fulfilled it should have been Solomon. We are told that his annual income was six hundred and sixty-six talents of gold '*not* including the revenues brought in by merchants and traders' (2 Chron. 9.13). In present day terms this is about twenty-five tons of gold per year, which bearing in mind that gold currently sells at over 400 dollars an ounce, is an enormous amount. He had 700 wives, 300 concubines, and untold possessions, including 12,000 horses (2 Chron. 9.25). He had the type of wealth and possessions which the world suggests adds up to total happiness. He was no on-looker either. He spent his life actively pursuing pleasure, education, possessions and fame. Yet as he became older he learned that what Scripture taught was correct – that, in the long-run, whatever fallen man does he is left unfulfilled and empty. He expresses it very well in Ecclesiastes 2.11 'Yet when I surveyed all that my hands had done and what I had toiled to achieve, everything was meaningless, a chasing after wind; nothing was gained under the sun'.

The good news for the world is that God, who is above the sun, intervened into this quagmire of despair and masterminded a plan that would outwit the devil, defuse the fall and open a gateway of satisfaction and fulfilment to all who would choose his way.

The announcement of God's counter-offensive was made immediately after the fall of Adam. How like our God to declare his outright victory at the very time he seemed to have suffered an humiliating defeat. Genesis 3, which reveals the fact of the fall, also reveals the answer to it. It is found in the passage where God outlines the effects of the fall on the serpent, the woman and the man and, because we are primarily concerned here with the curse on the serpent, we'll look at them in reverse order.

As far as man was concerned, as we have seen in Chapter 2, one of the results of the fall was to be that creation would rebel against him and that he would find the ground only responding to hard work (v17–19).

For the woman the remembrance of the fall was to be in her own body. She, who hoped to find fleshly delight in the fruit, would instead experience pain. 'Unto the woman he said "I will greatly multiply thy sorrow and thy conception; in sorrow thou shalt bring forth children; and thy desire shall be to thy husband, and he shall rule over thee"' (Genesis 3.16 KJV). This defines a number of consequences. The best known of which is that woman would experience a strange dilemma – while suffering pain in childbirth, she would still desire to bear more children.

But actually the pain which would be her portion is much more than pain in child-bearing; a female is more prone to mental, physical and spiritual pain than the male. This is the reason why Peter tells husbands to 'be considerate as you live with your wives and treat them with respect as the weaker partner' (1 Peter 3.7). Husbands must take into account the historical reality of the effects of the fall. How few men really understand the deep difference the fall has made in men and women, and no wonder that some partners are seen by their wives as brutish and inconsiderate in their behaviour.

Another consequence concerns her rôle – she, who sought to act independently of Adam, now found in herself a continual attraction and need for him which has become the universal lot of women.[1] Ardent feminists who try to deny this and stamp it out are attempting the impossible. Because of the independence displayed at the fall, the husband would now be the 'head' of his wife and would bear the rule.

It is, however, the word spoken to the serpent which really concerns us. Snakes arouse a sense of revulsion in the majority of people: their very movement and 'feel' are repulsive to many, and an aura of evil seems to accompany them. Genesis 3.14 says 'Cursed are you above all the livestock and all the wild animals! You will crawl on your belly and you will eat dust all the days of your life'. Why did God so curse a creature who was, after all, only the agent through which the real enemy worked? The Bible shows that the land and animals often share in the consequences of God's judgment. Where an animal was used in an act of abomination, for example, it was to be killed together with the man who had used it. Chrysostom explains it by saying that God does it 'just as a loving father, when punishing the murderer of his son might snap in two the sword or dagger with which the murder had been committed'.[2] Man's reaction to the reptile would serve as a constant reminder of the devil's reality and of the consequences of the fall. That it travels on its belly and eats food covered with dust reflects for us the power of God over the evil one and all his works.

The passage continues with God's words to Satan, who had used the serpent. Verse 15 says 'and I will put enmity between you and the woman, and between your offspring and hers; he will crush your head and you will strike his heel'. The picture of the snake is still much in evidence here. Snakes, with the exception of a few kinds, are confined to the ground and as a result their main attack is to strike at the feet of their human victim and inject poison into his (normally) life-bearing bloodstream. The instinctive reaction to such an attack is to attempt to crush the snake's head.

However the word 'enmity' reveals that this is not just a confrontation with an animal, for 'enmity' is something only personalities can experience whereas animals act by instinct rather than by conscious judgment. Once again the satanic power behind the scenes is revealed. The verse is a very interesting one and needs careful analysis.

At first the words are directed at only two characters: 'you' who is the devil; and 'the woman' who is Eve, but they continue prophetically to include 'your offspring' and 'hers'. The word 'offspring', or as the King James Version has it 'seed', is singular in the Hebrew, but it is a word which can be used as a collective noun. Such a word allows a singular to represent more than one and it is clear here that the devil's 'offspring' is not referring to one but many. Jesus shows this when he identifies the Jews who are planning to kill him as belonging to this group: 'You belong to your father, the devil, and you want to carry out your father's desire' (John 8.44). Similarly, when John the Baptist calls the Pharisees and Sadducees 'you brood of vipers', he is using the same imagery. All who oppose God's ways are included. Hence we know that 'your offspring' refers not to an individual but to a group which comprises all those beings, demonic and human, who resist God. As that is so, then it is clear that Eve's offspring must also refer to more than one. Of course, all human beings are her 'offspring' in the sense that all are descended from Adam and Eve, but here the term is very much more restricted, meaning those who would oppose and be at enmity with the devil. This is the 'little flock' of Luke 12.32 who are believers. The fall meant that they would always be at variance with the devil and his system. The New Testament bears this out: Jesus said to those who follow him 'If the world hates you, keep in mind that it hated me first. If you belonged to the world, it would love you as its own; as it is you do not belong to the world, but I have chosen you out of the world, that is why the world hates you' (John 15.18 and 19).

'Don't you know that friendship with the world is hatred towards God? Anyone who chooses to be a friend of the world becomes an enemy of God' (James 4.4).

As verse 15 continues, however, it then isolates and focuses upon one person, '*he* will crush your head, and you will strike his heel'. The devil had already struck at the heel of man and the venom of the fall was already circulating in man's veins, but here was one individual descendant of Eve who would fight not only the devil's offspring but the devil himself. As the problem came through the man, it is not surprising that the answer would come through the woman. Even today the Jewish feast of Passover reminds us of this, for it cannot begin until a woman symbolically lights a candle.

With the advantage of hindsight, and standing as we do with the fulfilment of the prophecy before us it is easy to know that Jesus Christ was the one spoken of here, but before his advent this verse would have been taken simply as saying that one would come, born of a woman, who would be the great conqueror and deliverer. He would be the champion of all believers and in him the whole of the believing population would find their centre and perfect expression. As the devil would fight for those who are his, so this man would fight for believers. This is why all Old Testament believers looked for the man who would come, and why John the Baptist was asked whether he was the one.

But we must look more carefully. This verse doesn't say that there will be a fight, it proclaims that there will be a resounding victory, with the devil crushed. At the very scene of human disaster God claims outright victory. No wonder this passage is called the 'Protevangel' or 'first proclamation of the gospel', for in one fell blow Satan's triumph is turned sour, and the victorious shrieking from hell is silenced. The exact details are left obscure, and this very obscurity is enough to make a mockery of the devil and force him to be constantly vigilant and defensive. Satan is *not* omniscient and the one mentioned in verse 15 could have meant to him any one of the woman's offspring who could come at any time in the future.

With the proclamation of God's eventual triumph still ringing in his ears Satan's fight now turned upon the believing descendants of Eve, for if he was to break God's word and thereby make him a liar, he had to destroy this man who was coming. As we trace his attacks we will see that the devil has been defeated right from the beginning.

It may be that Eve and Satan expected this man to appear very quickly and when Cain was born (Genesis 4.1) Eve says 'with the help of the Lord I have brought forth a man'. As it is translated here her remark is a prayer of praise and thanksgiving to God that the birth had been successful despite the pain, and certainly the name Cain which means 'Acquired' shows that she considered him a gift from God. It is worth noting that, despite the fall, her trust was now in the Lord, and he who had promised victory through her seed had been faithful in allowing her to have a male offspring. Some have translated the Hebrew as 'with the help of the Lord I have brought forth *the* man' and have concluded that Eve expected Cain to be the fulfilment of Genesis 3.15. That is doubtful, but clearly as far as she was concerned any one of her sons could have been the one.

As Satan assessed the character of Cain, and later of his brother Abel, he would have seen that Abel was much more likely than Cain to be the one promised. Their activity in offering sacrifices to God would have indicated that God had taught Adam and Eve that the shedding of blood was now the only way that sinful man could have communion with God. Genesis 3.7 tells us that when Adam and Eve knew they were naked they made loincloths of fig-leaves to cover their nakedness. However, fig-leaves were inadequate and didn't cover the sin that had led to the discovery of their nakedness. God had to show them what he justly required and Genesis 3.21 was an important lesson to them. The Lord removed their self-made coverings and, taking innocent animals, he killed and skinned them and from their skins made new loincloths. These were the first animals killed on the earth and their deaths were only necessary because of the fall. The lesson was very important – that without the shedding of blood fallen man is totally unacceptable to God and unable to approach him. What a seed-bed of revelation Genesis 3 is – we have already looked at the fall and at the triumph of God's plan and now the skin clothes speak to us pictorially of Calvary and of the end of time when all who believe will be clothed with garments of righteousness and immortal glory.

Certainly Cain and Abel knew all about offerings to God and knew from Adam that all such offerings required the shedding of blood. The killing of an innocent sacrifice in his place was man's acknowledgment that his sin deserved death and had to be covered before any of the works of his hands could be received. In Genesis 4.4 we read that Abel, who kept sheep, had not come with woollen or milk products which he made but with 'fat portions'. As we have seen, no meat was eaten on the earth at this time and this implies that Abel acknowledged the need for sacrifice. In comparison to this we find Cain bringing 'some fruits of the soil' but ignoring the lesson which God had taught to his parents. In effect, he refused to acknowledge that he was totally fallen and cast aside the righteous demands of God. An outward religiosity is no proof of one's devotion to God, for God looks upon the heart and sees whether it reflects the fear of the Lord, which is the beginning of wisdom.

It is no wonder, therefore, that God could not accept Cain's offering. As Hebrews 9.22 says 'without the shedding of blood there is no forgiveness'. His offering was not at all inferior to Abel's as far as we know, but Abel's was given with a blood sacrifice.

When Cain expressed his anger about the rejection of his offering God asks, 'why are you angry? Why is your face downcast? If you do what is right, will you not be accepted? But if you do not do what is right sin is crouching at your door' (Gen.4.6 and 7). The Hebrew word *chattah* (translated 'sin') means either 'sin' or 'sin-offering' and it is clearly the latter which should be used here. 'But if you do not what is right a sin-offering lies at the door'.

As Satan viewed this he realised that Cain was one of his offspring who opposed God's ways. 1 John 3.12 confirms it: 'Do not be like Cain who belonged to the evil one.' Abel was, therefore, the one through whom the danger might come. What more obvious path could there be for Satan than to cause Cain to rise up through jealousy and murder his brother? It was Cain's gesture of defiance – if God wanted a sacrifice, he would give him his brother Abel! With Abel gone, Satan might still achieve his aim.

Jesus certainly blames the devil for Abel's death; he declares that the devil 'was a murderer from the beginning' (John 8.44).

Needless to say, the devil was mistaken about Abel and when Eve had another son his vigilance was again vital. The birth of Seth re-established the godly line, indeed, the name Seth means 'substitute'. 'Adam lay with his wife again, and she gave birth to a son and named him Seth saying, "God has granted me another child in place of Abel, since Cain killed him."' (Gen.4.25). From the time of Seth right through to the birth of *the* man, Satan's main preoccupation was to prevent his coming, and whenever his exact line of descent was identified by the word of the Lord, Satan mounted an attack upon it.

The line is easy for us to trace. At the flood only Noah and his family were believers; the rest of the earth's population had rejected God and followed the devil; therefore, at that point, the 'seed of the woman' was represented by only eight people: Noah, his three sons Shem, Japheth and Ham and their respective wives. After God's judgment had destroyed the earth these were the people through whom the earth was to be repopulated. In Genesis 9.26 God identifies Shem, or the Semitic people, as being the ones through whom his champion would come. 'Blessed be the Lord, the God of Shem' is a statement which shows that God was going to entrust his revelation, his oracles and his ways to the descendants of Shem. All of God's plans were invested in the Semitic line and that included his plan to defeat Satan through the individual of Genesis 3.15.

Ten generations after Shem, Abraham was born, and God's word to him according to Genesis 12.3 was that 'all peoples on earth will be blessed through you.' By this time the Semitic peoples numbered millions, but God, through his word, indicated that his plan now passed down through this man whom he had sovereignly called from

Mesopotamia. It was easy for Satan to know that his son Isaac and grandson Jacob were part of the plan too, through the words God spoke about them.

Jacob's twelve sons, however, opened up the possibilities again. Perhaps Satan suspected that the line might continue through Joseph, in which case the plot by his brothers to kill him, thwarted only when Reuben objected (Gen. 37.21 and 22), may have been the arch-murderer plotting again. Actually it was Joseph's brother Judah through whom the line would pass. On his death-bed Jacob prophesied concerning each of his sons and to Judah he said 'The sceptre will not depart from Judah, nor the ruler's staff from between his feet, *until he comes to whom it belongs* and the obedience of nations is his' (Gen. 49.10). This was a clear statement that God had not forgotten his promise and that his plan was still on course. Judah himself was not the man, but certainly one of his descendants would be. From this time on Judah was viewed by all as the royal, kingly tribe.

Finally, ten generations after Judah, King David came to the throne. Then came the final announcement of the family into which the one who would represent the woman's seed would be born. In 2 Samuel 7.16 God promised David 'Your house and your kingdom shall endure forever before me; your throne shall be established forever.'

The man would be a descendant of Abraham through the royal Davidic line. Here is the King's Highway of history:-

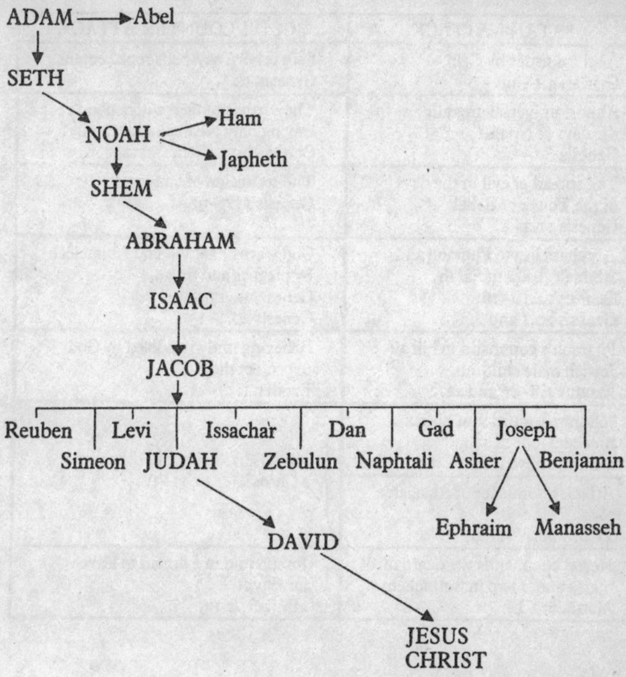

It was to be about 1000 years after David that God's time would come. 'But when the time had fully come, God sent his son, born of a woman, born under law, to redeem those under law that we might receive the full rights of sons' (Gal.4.4).

Despite all of Satan's attempts to stop it, God's word would be fulfilled. To show the constant humiliation and defeat of the devil during this period of waiting it will be of value for us to end this chapter by studying a few of the attacks that Satan made on the line of the Redeemer.

The table below outlines eight of the Satanic attacks on the line of Jesus with the counter-attack used by God to thwart them.

SATAN'S ATTACK	GOD'S COUNTER-ATTACK
Abel's murder by Cain Genesis 4.1–8.	Seth is born as Abel's replacement Genesis 4.25.
Almost universal ungodliness in the days of Noah Genesis 6.1–12.	The earth is judged with a flood leaving only Noah and his family Genesis 6.13–Genesis 7.24.
The spread of evil in the days of the Tower of Babel Genesis 11.1–6.	The confusion of languages Genesis 11.7–9.
Abraham lies to Pharaoh and Abimelech about Sarah Genesis 12.10–16; Genesis 20.1 and 2.	God warns Pharaoh and Abimelech by plagues and dreams Genesis 12.17–20; Genesis 20.3–15.
Pharaoh's command to kill all Jewish male children Exodus 1.8–16 and 22.	Believing midwives used by God to protect them Exodus 1.17–21.
Jehoram's murder of his six brothers 2 Chronicles 21.4.	Joash is hidden by Jehosheba 2 Chronicles 22.11–12.
Athaliah's murder of Ahaziah's sons 2 Chronicles 22.10	
Herod commands the death of all males under two in Bethlehem Matthew 2.16.	Joseph told in a dream to leave for Egypt Matthew 2.13.

A few of these will serve to demonstrate the principles involved.

Attack in Egypt

Israel suffered in Egypt on account of the Redeemer who was to come, for if Satan could exterminate the Jews then the plan of God would be thwarted. Much that we would put down to sheer human wickedness is actually satanically inspired and it is only when the full facts are known that the devil's fingerprints can be identified at the scene of the crime.

Exodus 1 describes the history of the Jews after Joseph's generation had died. 'Now Joseph and all his brothers and all that generation died, but the Israelites were fruitful and multiplied greatly and became exceedingly numerous, so that the land was filled with them' (verses 6 and 7).

The Pharaoh of that day who, the Bible tells us, 'did not know about Joseph' became concerned at the increase in numbers and decided to adopt a plan to reduce them. His plan was clearly that of the devil. At first, the Egyptians simply oppressed them and used them as slaves, but when that didn't stem their increase a new strategy had to be introduced.

'The king of Egypt said to the Hebrew midwives, Shiphrah and Puah, 'when you help the Hebrew women in childbirth and observe them on the delivery stool, if it is a boy kill him; but if it is a girl, let her live"' (vv 15 and 16). The effect is obvious: if Satan's enemy should come in that generation he would be killed as soon as he was born. If this plan were to succeed, then after only a few generations, the Jewish male line would be completely exterminated and Satan would be riding high on victory.

The plan was thwarted because the 'seed of woman' was still active and the enmity prophesied meant that those who were believers would reject the serpent's, and therefore Pharaoh's instructions. 'The midwives, however, feared God and did not do what the king of Egypt had told them to do; they let the boys live' (v 17).

As a result of this and other ploys, the male line of the Jewish families was preserved. The totality of the victory is clear when it is seen that God not only triumphed but even used the enemy to preserve the future Jewish deliverer, Moses. Moses' mother, desiring to protect her baby son from the persecution, made a waterproof basket to put him in and floated it along the Nile. God so moved that it passed the place where Pharaoh's daughter was bathing and she took him and brought him into the palace where he lived and grew up. Pharaoh himself protected the Jewish lad and ensured the future deliverance of the Jews. This is the first glimpse we have that God's purpose for his children is not only that they should be conquerors but that by his transcendent power they shall be more than conquerors.

Attack on the Davidic line

The most devastating attacks of the enemy on the line of David occurred in the days of Queen Athaliah. She is certainly one of the most evil women in the Bible, eclipsing even her mother Jezebel. In the days of David's grandson Rehoboam the Jewish nation had split into two parts – ten tribes formed the Northern Kingdom of Israel and the remaining two formed the Southern Kingdom of Judah. Athaliah's father, Ahab, was king of the Northern Kingdom, Israel, and the testimony of Scripture concerning him is that 'Ahab, son of Omri, did more evil in the eyes of the Lord than any of those before him. He not only considered it trivial to commit the sins of Jeroboam, son of Nebat, but he also married Jezebel, daughter of Ethbaal king of the Sidonians, and began to serve Baal and worship him' (1 Kings 16.30 and 31).

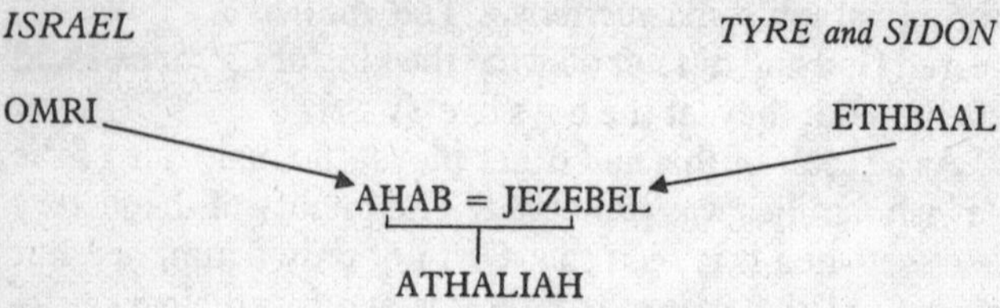

Ethbaal was a priest of Baal who came to the throne of Tyre by murdering the legitimate king whose name was Pheles. His daughter Jezebel was jealous to spread the worship of Baal, and after her marriage to Ahab her main mission in life was to stamp out the holy worship of Jehovah and murder his prophets. Behind her was Satan himself, seeking by this alliance with Ahab to destroy

God's people from the face of the earth. It was to this match that Athaliah was born.

In the Southern Kingdom of Judah a man called Jehoram had been appointed to the throne by his father Jehoshaphat, and it was through these descendants of David that the promised seed would come. There were altogether seven sons of Jehoshaphat and there had been much rivalry between them. Jehoram's first act was to kill all of his brothers, and before long he made matters even worse by marrying Ahab's daughter Athaliah. On the throne of Judah, therefore, was a murderer who was married to one of Baal's high priestesses.

This was a most critical period and a bottle-neck in the history of redemption. All the wonderful godly works of Jehoshaphat were undone in Jehoram's days and so great was the evil that finally God stirred up the Philistines and Arabians to come against him in judgment. 'They attacked Judah, invaded it and carried off all the goods found in the king's palace, together with his sons and wives. Not a son was left to him except Ahaziah, the youngest' (2 Chron. 21.17). God's judgment was so hot against Jehoram that he too soon died of an incurable disease of the bowels, leaving his last remaining son Ahaziah as the only one through whom the Redeemer could come.

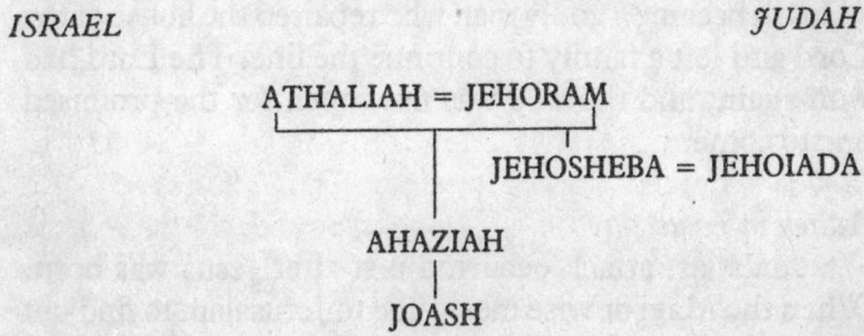

Even darker days were ahead. Ahaziah married and had sons by his wife and after only a year of being king he was killed while fighting with the king of Israel against the Syrians. It was at this moment that Satan saw his chance and with Ahaziah's mother, Athaliah, still alive he had the perfect servant ready to act. 2 Chronicles 22.10 tells us the fearful tale. 'When Athaliah the mother of Ahaziah saw that her son was dead, she proceeded to destroy the whole royal family of the house of Judah.' Here is the point at which Satan is within one blow of victory.

Once again God had a believer at hand to protect the line. While Athaliah was heartlessly killing her own grandchildren so that she could be the undisputed ruler, Jehosheba, the sister of Ahaziah and wife of the high priest Jehoida, took Ahaziah's youngest child, Joash, who was only one year old, and hid him. 'But Jehosheba, the daughter of King Jehoram and sister of Azahiah took Joash son of Ahaziah and stole him away from among the royal princes who were about to be murdered. She put him and his nurse in a bedroom to hide him from Athaliah; so he was not killed. He remained hidden with his nurse at the temple of the Lord for six years while Athaliah ruled the land' (2 Kings 11.2 and 3).

Only when Joash was seven did Jehoiada the priest publically reveal his presence and proclaim him king. At that moment the troops rebelled against Athaliah and put her to death.

Joash became a godly man who repaired the house of the Lord and left a family to continue the line. The Lord had won again, and the way was now open for the promised one to come.

Attack in Jesus' day

Satan's last attack occurred just after Jesus was born. When the Magi or wise men came to Jerusalem to find out where the king would be born, Herod asked them to report back to him when they had found him. He knew that there could only be one king and so this child had to be removed. Herod's reaction was that of a man eager to keep his throne and stop anyone else usurping it, but clearly behind it lay the serpent's desperate realisation that this was his last chance to destroy the man.

After the Magi had visited Bethlehem and seen the child, God warned them in a dream not to return to Herod, and at the same time he sent an angel to Joseph to tell him to take Mary and the baby Jesus to Egypt. A poor carpenter could never have afforded to do such a thing, but God who knows the end from the beginning had already made provision by the gift of gold from one of the Magi.

Knowing that time was short and that urgent action was necessary, Herod sent a command that all boys under the age of two in the Bethlehem area should be murdered. By the time the troops arrived to carry out the instruction, however, Joseph and his little family were safely on their way.

With the appointed Representative of the seed of the woman now on the earth the battle entered its final and deadliest stage.

4: Jesus Christ – pioneer of our victory

The good news that we have examined in the Old Testament is that despite his best endeavours Satan failed in his attempts to stop the birth of the promised Redeemer. Jesus Christ, who had been so long awaited, entered the dark arena of human history amid a fanfare of angelic jubilation. The testimony which they gave at his birth confirmed in every detail that this was the one prophesied as the man of Genesis 3.15.

'He will be great and will be called the Son of the Most High. The Lord God will give him the throne of his father David, and he will reign over the house of Jacob forever; his kingdom will never end' (Luke 1.32 and 33).

'Today in the town of David a Saviour has been born to you; he is Christ the Lord' (Luke 2.11).

He who was the Prince of Life and the Light of the world had come to redeem man from the guilt and power of sin and restore him, not only to his former position, but to one far higher. He had come to 'destroy the works of the devil' (1 John 3.8) and to 'crush' Satan's head as had been prophesied of him. The victory he would win would be so great that it would stand for all eternity, and though the devil would have the opportunity to fight back, 'the gates of hell would not prevail' against the work.

Let us remind ourselves of the problems which Jesus came to solve. The consequences of Adam's sin had been appalling: he who had been designed to have fellowship with God and enjoy all of creation was now separated by sin from the righteous God. Through sacrificing animals some contact was re-established but these sacrifices weren't enough to provide a permanent solution – as the writer to the Hebrews says, 'it is impossible for the blood of bulls and goats to take away sins.' The gulf seemed permanent and unbridgeable.

Moreover, man had become enslaved to sin. Through Adam sin had entered into man's basic make-up and had been passed on to everyone. Man was by nature a sinner and hence he was predisposed to commit sins. No human individual was free from this sinful state and therefore no one could be righteous before God. As God is a God of absolute justice, his very essence demands that sins be judged. Romans 6.6 declares the righteous verdict that: 'The wages of sin is death.' All who sin deserve to die both spiritually, which means separation from God, and physically.

Furthermore not one human being was capable of righteousness. Mankind had become, and still remains, so thoroughly tainted that even our 'good deeds are as filthy rags' (Isaiah 64.6) before God. Compared to his righteousness, ours is dirty black.

The devil must have been very confident. Through his subtlety man was away from God, in bondage to a sinful nature, constantly committing sins which would demand God's wrath and incapable of any righteousness which would be acceptable to God. In this circumstance he was surrounded by the results of the fall and subject to bondage, pain, fear and death.

Within thirty-three years of his birth Jesus would have broken this stranglehold and given man the choice of freedom. By his birth, his life and his death he would solve every problem confronting fallen man.

His birth

Jesus' birth immediately solved two basic problems. These are expressed admirably by Job, so we'll allow him to state them. The first concerns the separation between

God and man. 'He is not a man like me', says Job, 'that I might answer him, that we might confront each other in court. If only there was someone to arbitrate between us, to lay his hand upon us both, someone to remove God's rod from me, so that his terror would frighten me no more' (Job 9.32–34).

An arbitrator or mediator is someone who can fully represent both sides, and the phrase 'to lay his hand upon us both' speaks of the need for complete identification. Under the law a man had to offer an animal sacrifice to cover his sin but in Leviticus 3.2, and many other passages, the offerer was told to lay his hand on the animal's head before it was killed. This symbolised the fact that because of his sin he deserved to die, but that he was identifying fully with the animal so that it would die in his place.

Job saw clearly that as God is God, and man is man, the gulf was humanly impossible to bridge. As Jesus said, 'That which is born of the flesh is flesh; and that which is born of the spirit is spirit' (John 3.6 KJV). If there were to be a mediator for Job's cause he would have to be both God and man in one person, something which was inconceivable to Job.

The second problem that he saw clearly was that animal sacrifices could never remove the problem of sin and that, therefore, the coming Redeemer had to be a man. But being a man he would surely inherit the corruption of the fall and so be in as much bondage as we are; how could people who were imprisoned by the fall be helped by one who was as much a prisoner as they? If only all humans had such a clear understanding of this problem they would see the failure of all other religions and the uniqueness of Christianity.

'Who can bring a clean thing out of an unclean? Not one.'[1] (Job 14.4 KJV). Bildad expresses it even more precisely, 'How then can man be justified with God? or how can he be clean that is born of a woman?' (Job 25.4 KJV).

It is only the unique birth of Jesus which solves these two problems. The Gospels of Matthew and Luke reveal clearly that Jesus was conceived by the Holy Spirit and born of a virgin. This had been prophesied by Isaiah. In Isaiah 7.14 we read, 'The virgin will be with child and will give birth to a son, and will call him Immanuel.' The word 'virgin' in this Hebrew passage is *almah* which means both virgin and young woman; but in the Gospel account where this is quoted the Greek word *parthenos* is used, which can only mean 'virgin' (see Matthew 1.23). 'Immanuel' which is translated 'God with us' means much more than just 'being alongside', it means 'he became one of us'.

Being virgin-born solved the problem of the inherited fallen nature, for in by-passing the human father, Jesus was untainted by it. Mary herself was fallen as she confirms when she calls God her 'Saviour' in Luke 1.47, but the child she would bear is called 'the holy one' by the angel Gabriel in Luke 1.35. This child would not have the root of sin that all others had inherited. Many have thought of Jesus' sinlessness in terms of his freedom from committing any sins but that is not enough for he had to be born free from the sinful state as well. Without the virgin birth we have no ground at all for belief in the sinlessness of our Lord, for it alone explains why he was not born a sinner. It is our inborn fallen nature which gives Satan a head start in our lives and so it was essential that while born in the human manner Jesus was free from this defilement. Here at last was the free-man who could solve the sin problem. 'You know that he appeared so that he might take away our sins. And in him is no sin' (1 John 3.5). Job's second problem is answered in Christ.

So, thankfully, was the first. Because he was conceived by the Holy Spirit and born of the virgin Mary he combined and brought into union human and divine nature.

Jesus is God and man in one person. This had been understood from the first but was only officially formulated at the Council of Chalcedon in 451 AD. They expressed it beautifully: 'Jesus Christ is true humanity, undiminished Deity united in one person without confusion forever.' The wording may seem strange and yet every part is vital. If we deny his 'undiminished Deity' and thereby make him less than God then by definition he isn't God at all, and having fellowship with Jesus Christ would not be having fellowship with God but with less than God. Thus the old man Athanasius stood up and waved his finger at those who were attacking Christ's character and said, 'If Christ is *not* God, then we are not saved.'

In a similar way Jesus must be true humanity – for if we are all true humanity then if one is to die in our place he must be exactly like us. The price is high for making a mistake in this. Jesus is both God and man in one person – if he is not then we are saying that man and God can't be united and never will. The alternative is eternal separation and no salvation.

Why then did they add 'without confusion forever'? This is important and an example will explain it. When the colours yellow and blue are mixed together the result is neither yellow nor blue but green. That is what was meant by 'confusion'. So it is saying that in Jesus Christ God is still undiminished deity, and man is still true humanity – you do not have one who is a mixture of the two and therefore half God and half man. If he were he couldn't represent either God or man. The truth is that Jesus Christ was wholly God and wholly man and will remain so forever. The little baby blowing bubbles at his mother in his humanity, was at the same time holding the universe together in his divinity. If it were not so there would be no mediator, no redeemer and no saviour. The virgin-born God-man Jesus Christ alone solves man's problems.

'For there is one God and one mediator between God

and men, the man Christ Jesus' (1 Timothy 2.5). As both God and man Jesus represents God to man, and man to God. In him both sides are reconciled and the fulness of restored relationship can be seen clearly. Job would have been overjoyed to see the beautiful planning of God.

The virgin-birth then is not just of theological interest, it is of fundamental importance.[1] If it is a myth then there is no possible salvation for man, for the problems which Job saw so clearly would remain beyond solution. It also follows that 'salvation is found in no-one else, for there is no other name under heaven given to men by which we must be saved' (Acts 4.12).

His life

We have already seen the problem caused by the failure of the first Adam in the Garden of Eden when he chose to ignore God's revealed will and to give in to the will of the enemy, and it is clear that part of the work of Christ had to be the reversal and undoing of Adam's sin.

The first Adam was created sinless and the last Adam was born sinless but both began with the ability to choose and to be tempted. In Hebrews 10.5–7 we have a statement made by the Lord to his Father in which he rejoices to have been born a human being, 'Therefore when Christ came into the world, he said, 'Sacrifice and offering you did not desire, but a body you prepared for me; with burnt offerings and sin offerings you were not pleased. Then I said "Here I am – it is written about me in the scroll – I have come to do your will O God."' The offerings were only necessary because man had failed to obey God and so they constantly spoke to God of disobedience and failure. How much more would he have preferred obedience and loyalty. As Samuel said to King Saul, 'Does the Lord delight in burnt offerings and sacrifices as much as in obedience to the voice of the Lord? To obey is better than to sacrifice and to heed is better than the fat of rams' (1

Samuel 15.22). Adam failed to obey. Jesus, however, was coming with the mission of doing God's will perfectly. God would allow Satan to tempt Jesus just as he did the first Adam and Jesus' task was to overcome. 'I have come to do your will O God' expresses the whole purpose of Jesus' life.

Except for one short incident in the life of Jesus when he was twelve, we know few details of his life until the age of thirty. That he lived and worked as a carpenter and had at least four brothers and three sisters can be gleaned from passages like Matthew 13.55 and Mark 6.3, but of his personal life we know nothing. At the beginning of his ministry, however, when he was baptised by John the Baptist in the Jordan God personally testified of him that 'This is my Son, whom I love; with him I am well pleased' (Matt 3.17). God, who is absolutely righteous and holy, cannot tolerate the smallest hint of sin, and so this testimony shows that for the first thirty years of his life Jesus had met God's righteous standards absolutely. But it was undoubtedly in the last three and a half years of his life that he experienced the most severe testing.

Although he was born without a fallen nature he was still tempted and suffered through temptation just as we do. The testimony of Scripture is very clear: 'Because he himself suffered when he was tempted, he is able to help those who are being tempted' (Hebrews 2.18). 'For we do not have a high priest who is unable to sympathise with our weaknesses, but we have one who has been tempted in every way, just as we are – yet was without sin' (Hebrews 4.15). Indeed, as we shall see, he was tempted in ways we have never experienced and still came through without having deviated at all from his Father's will.

Everyone testified of his sinlessness. Towards the end of his ministry Jesus took Peter, James and John up on to the top of Mount Hermon and there he was transfigured before them so that his face shone and his clothes became exceedingly white and shining. Again the Father testified of his Son's perfection, saying, 'This is my Son, whom I love; with him I am well pleased. Listen to him' (Matthew 17.5).

Jesus' own life and words also confirmed his perfect keeping of God's will. Though he regularly visited the Temple he is never reported as having offered a sacrifice for his own sins, nor of confessing any. He prayed 'Father forgive them,' (Luke 23.34) but never 'Father, forgive me.' The wrongly named 'Lord's prayer' which includes the often repeated passage 'forgive us our trespasses as we forgive those who have trespassed against us' was taught to the disciples and was for them to pray. We have no record that Jesus prayed it himself.

Jesus said of his own life before the Father, 'I always do what pleases him' (John 8.29), and of those standing around he asked, 'can any of you prove me guilty of sin?' (John 8.46).

Even enemies testified of his holiness. Demons said of him, 'I know who you are – the Holy One of God!' His betrayer and accusers knew he was innocent. Judas, after his awful deed, confirms 'I have sinned . . . for I have betrayed innocent blood' (Matt. 27.4). He had been with Jesus for three and a half years and knew he was guiltless. Pilate could find 'no basis for a charge against him' (John 19.4) and his wife warns him to have nothing to do 'with that innocent man' (Matthew 27.19). None of his accusers could agree about what he had done and one of the thieves crucified with him while certain of his own guiltiness rebuked the other thief with the words, 'We are punished justly for we are getting what our deeds deserve. But this man has done nothing wrong' (Luke 23.41). Finally the centurion who acted as his executioner was convinced, saying, 'Surely this was a righteous man' (Luke 23.47).[2]

Despite all the temptations of the enemy and the pressure and oppression from those around him Jesus did his

Father's will completely. He knew exactly what pressure and suffering he would experience at his trial and crucifixion, and the anticipation of the Cross lay constantly before him casting a dark shadow over his earthly path. Perhaps the greatest test was in the Garden of Gethsemane. The account of his prayer shows exactly how intense the pressure became. The physician Luke tells us what happened. 'He withdrew about a stone's throw beyond them, knelt down and prayed "Father, if you are willing, take this cup from me; yet not my will but yours be done." And being in anguish he prayed more earnestly and his sweat was like drops of blood falling to the ground' (Luke 22.41, 42 and 44). The sweating of blood occurs when a person is under intense emotional stress[3] and many examples in modern times have been documented. In his 'Commentary on the Four Gospels' published in 1639 Joannes Maldonatus[4] tells of a healthy young man who, on hearing he had been sentenced to death, became bathed in a bloody sweat. A French historian[5] reports that King Charles IX of France also had a discharge of such sweat during his last illness on May 8th 1574. Most of us have never been under this type of pressure but Jesus went through it at its worst so that he could identify with and stand in for all humanity.[6]

He also underwent trials which none of us can experience. We have already examined the fact that he was wholly God and wholly man in one person, but Philippians 2.6–8 tells us that, 'Christ Jesus, who being in very nature God, did not consider equality with God something to be grasped, but made himself nothing, taking the very nature of a servant, being made in human likeness. And being found in appearance as a man, he humbled himself and became obedient to death – even death on a cross.' This passage does not mean that while on earth Jesus ceased to be divine; as we have seen he is God forever. What it does mean is that while on earth he gave up the right to express his divinity outwardly so that he who was master of the universe, high above all and glorious, appeared to those around him as a servant subject to his Father's will. He was willing to be born into a poor family in poor surroundings, to become a carpenter, to be despised and rejected of men and in every way to be totally identified with the human condition. He who was omniscient 'grew in wisdom and stature and in favour with God and men' (Luke 2.52) and spoke only the words of his Father. He who was omnipresent was confined to only one place at a time. He who was omnipotent experienced weariness (John 4.6), hunger (Matthew 4.2), thirst (John 19.28) and performed miracles only by the power of the Holy Spirit. The words quoted by Bishop Christopher Wordsworth bear repeating: 'He was hungry as a man and yet He is the Bread of Life, athirst He was as a man, and yet He says, Let him that is athirst come to Me and drink. He was weary and is our Rest; He was weighed down with sleep and yet is buoyed upon the sea. He pays tribute and is a King; He is called a Devil and casts out devils; prays and hears prayer; weeps and dries our tears; is sold for thirty pieces of silver, and redeems the world; is led as a sheep to the slaughterer, and is the Good Shepherd; is mute like a sheep, and is the Everlasting Word; is the Man of Sorrows, and heals our pains; is nailed to a tree and dies upon it and by the tree restores us to life; has vinegar to drink and changes water into wine; lays down His life and takes it again; dies and gives life and by dying destroys death.'[7]

Matthew 4.1–11 records the ways in which the devil tempted him after he had been fasting for forty days and forty nights in the desert. So rich and fruitful is this passage of Scripture that in many ways we can all identify with Jesus in these temptations, but the first two were really a subtle ploy to tempt him to use his divine attributes to relieve his human condition. Had they been successful he would have failed in his task. In the first temptation Satan said, 'If you are the Son of God, tell these stones to become bread' (Matthew 4.3) and in the second Satan took him up to a pinnacle of the Temple and said, 'If you are the Son of God throw yourself down' (v6). Jesus could make stones into bread very easily, and would have survived throwing himself from the roof of the Temple, but the people with whom he came to identify could have done neither and so it was imperative for him to resist the temptation and to suffer in every way like them.

Needless to say, by obeying the will of his Father, Jesus completely fulfilled the Law and it is important for us to understand what this life of obedience achieved. Hebrews 2.10 says, 'In bringing many sons to glory, it was fitting that God, for whom and through whom everything exists should make the Pioneer of their salvation perfect through suffering.' This does not deny the initial sinlessness of Christ but rather shows that he succeeded where Adam failed. Adam was created sinless but became a sinner when he failed to meet the test God put upon his free-will. The potential he lost was fully realised in Jesus who resisted temptation and overcame the tempter. In thus fulfilling the ideal of the Creator, he became man in the image of God, the 'last Adam', the delight of his Father's heart.

His righteousness is vital to us because salvation involves much more than the removal or subtraction of sin. A sinner minus his sins is still not good enough, for the saving of a soul requires the positive addition of absolute righteousness to the sinner for him to meet and have fellowship with God. Through Jesus' life that righteousness became freely available to us.

Still further, the fulfilment of the Law has brought an open window of blessing by removing the inevitable curse of the broken covenant. God said of his commandments that blessings would follow if they were obeyed, but that cursing was the result of their being neglected (Deut. 28.1–14 cf Deut. 28.15–68). In Jesus' complete fulfilment of the Law the full blessings of God have become available for us richly to enjoy.

With his righteousness shining as the sun, he was now ready for the final showdown with the enemy in which he would defeat and disarm the devil once and for all.

His death

It is important for us to realise that the death of Jesus on the cross of Golgotha is the very heart of the Gospel message and were we to preach everything else and ignore the Cross we would miss the very soul and substance of our salvation. How many there are today who see the works and blessings which are ours in Christ, and yet who have never fully realised and been humbled by the torment which Jesus experienced when he died in our place on the Cross. Selfishness, self-righteousness, ingratitude, unlovingness and many other attitudes which beset Christians vanish like a mist at the foot of Calvary and it is vital for us to go back to it regularly in our meditations.

God is so holy that he cannot look upon sin. Where it occurs it must be cursed and those who have committed it punished: 'The soul that sinneth, it shall die' (Ezekiel 18.4 KJV) and 'The wages of sin is death' (Romans 6.23) are two of the many statements which tell us the penalty and result of sin. Mankind is, therefore, under God's curse and subject to his wrath and in each generation the problem has been increased. Unless man is freed from the curse and penalty demanded by God's righteousness and justice, he can never have salvation in any form.

Jesus came to solve this problem by dying as our substitute. As Abraham and his son Isaac climbed Mount Moriah to sacrifice before the Lord, Isaac was puzzled to know from where the sacrifice would come and his father answered prophetically, 'God himself will provide' (Genesis 22.8). Jesus was God's answer. As God cannot die it was necessary for Jesus, God the Son, to come into the world as a man and his human birth was the means by which the sacrifice was made available. Jesus was born into the world for the express purpose of dying and when John the Baptist saw him approaching he pointed at him and said, 'Look, the Lamb of God, who takes away the sin of the world!' (John 1.29). The sacrificial lamb had to be innocent, 'without blemish' (Exodus 12.5 KJV), and Jesus' sinless life made him the only man qualified to be the sacrifice to save the world.

When Jesus was crucified there was nothing he had done to deserve this punishment. Though spotless, he suffered in his own person the curse and penalty which was due to us, becoming our substitute that we might go free. He paid the penalty in full.

'Christ redeemed us from the curse of the law and by becoming a curse for us, for it is written: "Cursed is everyone who is hanged on a tree"' (Gal. 3.13).

He 'gave himself for our sins' (Gal. 1.4).

'He himself bore our sins in his body on the tree' (1 Peter 2.24). Nowhere is God's love for us shown more powerfully. There are those today who speak and act as if God can just overlook sin or be lenient towards it and they usually emphasise the fact that God is love and exclude or ignore his other characteristics. If it were true, then the Cross would be unnecessary and Jesus' death would be meaningless and unspeakably cruel. But they are wrong and have been deceived by a lie of the devil, who is a liar from the beginning. At the Cross the truth is revealed and God's love, righteousness and justice dovetail together. God must punish every sin but has shown his love by providing the answer. 'God so loved the world that he gave his one and only Son that whosoever believes in him shall not perish but have eternal life' (John 3.16). It was God who placed our sins on his Lamb that his character might be satisfied and his wrath placated that we might gain full and free access to him.

'The Lord has laid on him the iniquity of us all' (Isaiah 53.6).

'God made him who had no sin to be sin for us, so that in him we might become the righteousness of God' (2 Cor.5.21).

No man can know the true depth of suffering Jesus endured on the Cross. Although we have no direct account it is clear that during the six hours Jesus suffered on the Cross, the devil and his demons would have mounted a terrible assault upon the Saviour. How great must have been the temptation to use his divine power to come down and stop the taunts of the enemy and his seed and openly confound them, but had he done so humanity would have been consigned permanently to outer darkness. This would have been tantamount to taking of the tree of life without first destroying the effects of the tree of knowledge of good and evil. But Jesus had a higher way set before him, therefore 'he endured the cross, scorning its shame' (Hebrews 12.2).

During the brutal and savage torture which the soldiers inflicted upon him, he uttered no sound but was like a lamb led to the slaughter. The first scream to come from his lips came only when the sins of the whole world, yours and mine, were laid upon him and God turned his back. The darkness which descended upon Jerusalem at that point was to stop all human eyes prying into the torment he experienced when he was plunged into separation from the one who had always sustained and upheld him. 'My God, My God, why have you forsaken me?' (Matthew 27.46) was his cry as spiritual death descended upon him. He was separated and left alone so that no other human being need ever be cut off from God again. No one is ever left or forsaken now; God is always there at our right hand 'a very present help in trouble' (Ps. 46.1 KJV).

No sin can ever be bigger than God's provision in Christ. Because Jesus Christ is God, the value of the life he laid down for us is infinite and the blood of Jesus represents the value in full. No sin is so terrible that it is not paid for. 'For you know that it was not with perishable things such as silver and gold that you were redeemed . . . but with the precious blood of Christ, a lamb without blemish or defect' (1 Peter 1.18 and 19). He paid for us by his blood and thereby showed our infinite value in his sight. 'This is love: not that we loved God, but that he loved us and sent his Son as an atoning sacrifice for our sins' (1 John 4.10).

To refuse his provision in Christ is to reject the only means of salvation, for there is no other sacrifice which solves our problems. 'How shall we escape if we ignore such a great salvation?' (Hebrews 2.3).

The first Adam had brought misery and tears, enslavement and the reign of sin and death. The last Adam brought love, joy and peace, freedom to become sons and royal priests, and replaced sin and death with the reign of grace and eternal life.

Before we leave the discussion of Jesus' physical death it is worth pausing to consider why he had to be crucified. Although crucifixion was unknown in King David's day the Holy Spirit had used him to prophesy about it. Psalm 22.16 says, 'they have pierced my hands and my feet.' One thousand years later crucifixion was in common use. The Romans of Jesus' day had copied crucifixion from the Carthaginians, who had adopted it originally from the Persians. It appealed to the ancient peoples because of its sheer cruelty in producing a long, slow death. Many would endure for days, crying out to passers-by to be merciful and kill them. The desperation of a man longing to die and yet unable to do so was so much more sadistic than beheading or stoning in which death occurred immediately.

Crucifixion was the only instrument which could have

satisfied God's demands. Jesus made it clear that his death would be a voluntary laying down of his life, when in John 10.18 he said, 'No-one takes it from me, but I lay it down of my own accord.' If Jesus had been beheaded or stoned then other men clearly would have taken his life. Through crucifixion, and crucifixion alone, Jesus could die as he wanted, *on* the Cross but not *of* the Cross. It is worth noting that the devil, realising this, would have tried to kill Jesus before he ever reached the Cross so that he could break the word of God and prove him a liar. It was the enemy who, on more than one occasion, caused crowds to seek to stone Jesus. When possible he hid from them (John 8.59) and when that was impossible he miraculously 'walked right through the crowd' (Luke 4.28–30). He had to fulfil the word of God. On the journey from his trials and torture to the Cross the satanic pressure on him must have been enormous. It was customary for the prisoner to carry his cross and normally Jesus, who had the muscles and shoulders of a carpenter, would have had no difficulty. After his torture, however, he was much weakened. When he stumbled God had already arranged for Simon of Cyrene to be there to make sure that Golgotha was reached. If no one had been there the Romans would have put him to death by the sword. It was only when the nails finally went into him that Satan's plans were utterly thwarted.

After six hours on the Cross Jesus' work was complete – He had satisfied God's righteous demands, paid in full for man's sins and had undone all that Adam had caused. His shout 'It is finished' (John 19.30) was a cry of total and complete victory and marked the fulfilment of the plan of God. All the opposition and attack of the enemy had come to nought, and the battle was now decisively won. The echo of that cry will last for eternity. Even today it rings out horrifyingly for the devil but triumphantly and full of hope for fallen humanity.

With the work done there was no reason for him to remain, and with his last breath he said words which confounded and amazed the Roman soldiers standing at the foot of the Cross. 'Jesus called out with a loud voice, "Father, into your hands I commit my spirit." When he had said this, he breathed his last' (Luke 23.46).

Never before had a crucified man been able to decide when he was to die. 'When the centurion and those with him who were guarding Jesus saw . . . what happened they were terrified and exclaimed, "Surely he was the Son of God"' (Matt. 27.54). The Prince of Life had just outwitted and outmanoeuvered death itself and demonstrated that it had no power over him. As Jesus died an earthquake thundered in the city; the rocks cried out in praise and stones rolled away from the tombs in testimony to the defeat of death itself. 'At that moment the curtain of the temple was torn in two from top to bottom' (Matt. 27.51). That curtain, which was sixty feet long and thirty feet wide and believed by some to be four inches thick, had stood for many centuries as a testimony of the separation between God and man. Now, as the priests busied themselves with their spiritually bankrupt religious duties, the curtain began to tear as a testimony to them. Man had been reconciled to God.

As the sun began to shine again and as the flowers re-opened and the birds resumed their songs, a new era of grace dawned across the world.

5: The glorified man

As we progress in our study of the victory Jesus has given us, there is nothing more important than that we should realise that when Jesus cried out from the Cross 'It is finished' he meant exactly what he said. Perhaps no other revelation is as essential as the finished work of Jesus on the Cross, for without it a believer can find himself on the wrong footing in the Christian life, and taken in by the devil's suggestions that the work was not thorough enough to cover him.

In John's Gospel there is a three-fold witness to the completed work, and the same Greek word is used in every verse.

'I have brought you glory on earth by *completing* the work you gave me to do' (John 17.4).

'Later, knowing that all was now *completed* . . . Jesus said, 'It is *finished*' (John 19.28 and 30).

From the very beginning, before the foundation of the world, until the end when all shall be presented to the Father in faultless perfection in glory, the plan of God centres entirely in the work of him who is mighty to save, and it is never stated or implied in Scripture that man can add materially to it. All we can do is believe that it avails for us. As Paul and Silas said to the jailer, 'Believe in the Lord Jesus and you will be saved' (Acts 16.31). To us who believe, Christ's finished work is reckoned in full and we have peace with God.

Everything that followed the Cross revealed and made available to us the accomplishments of Jesus on the cross, but it is the Cross itself which is the climax of God's work.

It was there that our total salvation was won, and there that our enemy the devil and his forces were humiliated. 'He forgave us all our sins, having cancelled the written code, with its regulations, that was against us and that stood opposed to us; he took it away, nailing it *to the cross*. And having disarmed the powers and authorities, he made a public spectacle of them, triumphing over them *by the cross*' (Col. 2.13–15). It was all accomplished when he died.

Romans 4.25 shows that even his resurrection occurred because of his completed work on the Cross, 'who was delivered up *because of* (for) our transgressions and was raised *because of* (for) our justification' (Wuest Expanded Translation). When Jesus entered the realm of death as a man, he knew that because of his own work of justification it could have no power over him, and that he could rise from the dead whenever he wanted. What greater evidence could he give to an unbelieving world that he was indeed the Messiah, and had truly accomplished all that had been prophesied of him?

As he travelled around Jerusalem and elsewhere he had been very specific concerning what would happen to him at the end of his ministry. 'The Son of Man is going to be betrayed into the hands of men. They will kill him, and on the third day he will be raised to life' (Matthew 17.22 and 23). 'We are going up to Jerusalem, and the Son of Man will be betrayed to the chief priests and the teachers of the law. They will condemn him to death and will turn him over to the Gentiles to be mocked and flogged and crucified. On the third day he will be raised to life!' (Matthew 20.18 and 19).

These predictions were not expressed privately but were known by thousands of people who were therefore very keen to see whether they would be fulfilled. Because of Jesus' words the chief priests went to Pilate after his death and asked for a guard to be posted at his tomb, reasoning that 'Otherwise, his disciples may come and steal the body and tell the people that he has been raised from the dead. This last deception will be worse than the first' (Matthew 27.64). The whole city talked of little else: when the two on the road to Emmaus met and talked with Jesus and he said to them, 'what are you discussing together as you walk along?', they replied, 'Are you the only one living in Jerusalem who doesn't know the things that have happened there in these days?' (Luke 24.17 and 18).

The first predictions had been fulfilled – he was delivered up and condemned in Jerusalem and he had been put to death. Was it possible that he would rise?

Although they didn't realise it, by asking for a guard to be put on the tomb, the chief priests were acting as God's agents to confirm the truth of the Resurrection. Pilate did not send the temple guards to stand by the tomb, but highly trained Roman soldiers who had all sworn allegiance to their Emperor. We can only wonder what passed through Pilate's mind when the very ones who had accused Jesus of plotting to destroy the Temple and build another in three days (Mark 14.57 and 58; Mark 15.29) now admitted that they had understood all along that Jesus had been referring to his own body. We are not told how many soldiers were posted but to satisfy the chief priests the number must have been substantial. The people of Jerusalem would have talked of nothing else – that fully armed Roman soldiers were guarding the tomb of Jesus in case some totally untrained and dispirited Galilean fishermen might steal the body!

When Jesus rose from the dead, he sent an angel to roll the stone away from the mouth of the tomb so that everyone could see he had risen. When this angel appeared with an accompanying earthquake 'The guards were so afraid of him that they shook and became like dead men' (Matthew 28.4). The guards must have known beyond doubt that Jesus was the Great Redeemer. When they came round they went into the city and told the chief priests what had happened. The chief priests found themselves in an awful dilemma. Even though they knew beyond a shadow of a doubt that Jesus had risen, they had to protect their own religious position and so had to spread a lie to explain the lack of a body. Few options were left to them. They couldn't say that the Galileans had fought with and beaten the soldiers and stolen the body – no-one would believe that. All they could do was to say that the soldiers had slept on duty. With large sums of money they bribed the soldiers to repeat this and promised that if the governor heard of it they wouldn't get into trouble. To the ordinary citizens it was an amazing tale: first of all, proud Roman soldiers just didn't sleep on duty. Secondly, the moving of the large stone would have made enough noise to awaken them. Thirdly, sleeping on duty was a capital offence in the Roman army and yet these soldiers went unpunished. Many of the people must have considered seriously that Jesus really had risen from the dead.

Furthermore, it wasn't long before people began to claim that Jesus had appeared physically to them. Altogether seventeen post-resurrection appearances of Jesus are listed in the Bible, of which eleven occurred just after he rose. These eleven are as follows:- (1) He appeared to Mary Magdalene (John 20.11–18); (2) to the women (Matthew 28.9–10); (3) to Peter (Luke 24.34); (4) to the disciples on the road to Emmaus (Luke 24.13–35); (5) to the disciples without Thomas (John 20.19–24); (6) a week later to the disciples and Thomas (John 20.26–29); (7) to the seven disciples by the sea of Galilee (John 21.1–23); (8) to over five hundred at one time (1 Cor. 15.6), most of whom were still alive when Paul wrote his first letter to the Corinthians; (9) to James, the Lord's brother (1 Cor. 15.7); (10) to his disciples on the mountain in Galilee (Matthew 28.16–20); and (11) to the disciples when he was taken up from the Mount of Olives (Luke 24.44–53).

Add to this the transformed lives of the disciples and the fact that within two months of his Master's death, Peter was able to convince three thousand people of the truth of the Resurrection (Acts 2.41), and it is clear that this was no fabrication. Peter said to the crowd, 'This man was handed over to you by God's set purpose and foreknowledge; and you, with the help of wicked men, put him to death by nailing him to the cross. But God raised him from the dead, freeing him from the agony of death because it was impossible for death to keep its hold on him' (Acts 2.23 and 24). His audience had been given ample opportunity to examine the evidence. Many of them had witnessed the death of Jesus and would have known whether Peter's words were mere fiction. But they believed.

The phrase 'it was impossible for death to keep its hold on him' expresses the Resurrection beautifully. An American friend of mine told me that this passage reminded him of the days when he would try to swim down to the bottom of the deep end of a swimming-pool with a cork board. It was impossible to keep it down. Jesus had been an uninvited visitor to the realm of death, and death had nothing to hold on to in him. After three days, when he who was eternal life decided to rise, death could do nothing about it. Some had been raised from the dead before, for example Lazarus (John 11.1–44) and the widow of Nain's son (Luke 7.11–17), but their escape from death was temporary and within a few years they died again. Jesus' resurrection was permanent and was the forerunner of a universal resurrection, which by the end of time would leave death without one person enslaved. For all humanity will be resurrected, some to eternal life and some to condemnation.

No other religious leader has ever made such bold claims and then risen from the dead to support them. The tomb of Mohammed at Mecca is still a centre of pilgrimage; so is the tomb of Gautama Buddha; so is the tomb of Jesus in Jerusalem. The difference is that Jesus' tomb is empty and he is still revealing himself today, whereas nothing has been heard from the others since their deaths. His Resurrection testifies to his work and is the guarantee that our sins are forgiven and that we too will be raised.

Before we study the Ascension, it is worth asking what Jesus did during the three days he spent in the realm of death. When the thief on the cross asked Jesus to remember him when he came into his kingdom, Jesus replied, 'I tell you the truth, today you will be with me in paradise' (Luke 23.43). The word 'paradise' came from a Persian word meaning 'garden of the king', and it was the name given in the Bible to the place where believers were sent when they died. There were people who lived before Jesus' day, and who had become believers because they had listened to and believed the testimony of Moses and the Prophets. The general words 'hell' and 'sheol' simply meant the 'unseen place' where the dead went, and within them there were separate places where believers and unbelievers were confined. In Luke 16.22 paradise is also called 'Abraham's side' or 'bosom' (KJV). It is into this place that the soul of Jesus descended when he died. He went there to announce to the believers – Adam and Eve, Job, Abraham, David and Daniel among them – that their faith had been rewarded and that the sins which formerly had only been covered were now removed through his work. It was a message of victory and triumph which announced to them that the way to heaven and into God's presence had been opened up. Within a few days, as we shall see, they had gone to be face to face with the Lord in heaven.

It is to the Ascension that we must now turn, for the Ascension was the means by which the victory Jesus had won was passed on to the Church.

While it is true that Jesus was visibly moved from the

earth into heaven forty days after he rose, it is possible that he also ascended into heaven and returned the very day of his resurrection. This certainly will surprise some, but it can be seen from the conversation between Jesus and Mary outside the tomb. 'She turned herself back, and saw Jesus standing, and knew not that it was Jesus. Jesus saith unto her, "Woman, why weepest thou? whom seekest thou?" She, supposing him to be the gardener, saith unto him, "Sir, if thou hast borne him hence, tell me where thou hast laid him, and I will take him away.' Jesus saith unto her, "Mary." She turned herself, and saith unto him, "Rabboni" which is to say, "Master".

Jesus saith unto her, "Touch me not; for I am not yet ascended to my Father: but go to my brethren and say unto them, I ascend unto my Father, and your Father; and to my God, and your God"' (John 20.14–17 KJV).

The use of the present tense 'I ascend' or 'I am ascending' would suggest that on that morning Jesus went up to the Father and returned to be with the disciples on the evening of that same day. Certainly it explains a number of mysteries. Why did Jesus tell Mary not to touch him, and yet a week later invite Thomas to put his finger into the nail prints and his hand into the wound in his side? It was certainly not through lack of affection, because the name he used, which should more accurately be translated 'Miriam', was the original Aramaic name by which her parents and friends would have addressed her. Jesus explains that she mustn't touch because 'I am not yet ascended to my Father.' Having won the victory Jesus had first to go and present his work to the Father, so that he received all the glory for it. Having gone up to the Father, he was then free to let Thomas touch him.

Also, it solves the problem some people have about the Holy Spirit. When Jesus appeared to the disciples on the evening of that day 'he breathed on them and said, "Receive the Holy Spirit"' (John 20.22). In John 16.7, however, Jesus had clearly told the disciples that it was 'for your good that I am going away. *Unless I go away*, the Counsellor will not come to you; but if I go, I will send him to you.' It would seem, therefore, that between his resurrection and his appearance to the disciples he had ascended.

The description of Jesus in 1 Corinthians 15.20 as the first-fruits of those who had fallen asleep bears this out further. When Israel entered the promised land and the manna ceased, the Lord instituted an official feast called the Feast of Firstfruits based upon the command whereby the Jews were required to give the first of their harvest to the Lord. As they didn't know how big the total crop of, say, grapes was going to be, giving the first-ripe grapes was always a step of faith. The feast was held just after Passover and marked the beginning of the fifty-day period leading up to Pentecost. Leviticus 23.10 says of it: 'When you enter the land I am going to give you and you reap its harvest, bring to the priest a sheaf of the first grain you harvest. He is to wave the sheaf before the Lord so that it will be accepted on your behalf.' It marked the beginning of the grain harvest when the first sheaves of barley (the earliest cereal to ripen) were ready to be cut. Once cut, the sheaf was taken to the priest who first waved it from side to side to show that it represented the whole harvest, and then before the Lord. It was raised up and brought straight down again. After that had happened the harvest was gathered in: after the barley the fruit; after the fruit the olives; after the olives the vines and, just before Pentecost, the wheat.

The first-fruit was offered to give God all the glory for the harvest about to be cut, and to pray for a greater harvest in the future. When Jesus rose he was the first-fruits of the harvest already waiting to be gathered in. Indeed the harvest was gathered in with him, for as he ascended he led into heaven the Old Testament believers whom he had visited during his three days in death. Not only were they transferred to heaven but so was Paradise itself. When Paul writes of heavenly visions in 2 Corinthians 12.3, he says 'this man . . . was caught *up* into Paradise.' This is why when believers die today they no longer descend, but go immediately up into heaven. The gulf of separation between God and man which had seemed so unbridgeable to Job had been closed forever. As Jesus ascended these believers ascended too. An even greater harvest, the Church, was yet to come. The old harvest began in defeat, and ended in victory, but the new harvest began in victory and will end in glory.

Ephesians 4.8 testifies of these things: 'when he ascended on high, he led captives in his train and gave gifts to men.' The picture Paul is employing here is one which was very familiar in his day. After the Roman armies had conquered a country they put on a spectacular for the people back at home. Before television and photography there was no way in which ordinary Roman citizens could visualise the captured territory or its inhabitants. Therefore the triumphant troops would bring back as many captives as possible and as much booty as they could carry to show the type of people they had been fighting against. As the army processed through the streets the citizens would cheer and many would receive gifts brought back from the war. However, when Jesus ascended, the captives he led were his own people whom he had won and angels cheered in the streets of heaven at the spectacle.

But it is we, the members of the Church, who have been showered with the spoils of his victory. So great were the results that we are constantly being surprised and delighted by what the Lord Jesus has provided for us.

These things may now give us an insight into the fascinating events recorded in Matthew 27.51. The passage refers to the time of Jesus' death but relates one incident which followed his resurrection. 'At that moment the curtain of the temple was torn in two from top to bottom. The earth shook and the rocks split. The tombs broke open and the bodies of many holy people who had died were raised to life. They came out of the tombs, and *after Jesus' resurrection* they went into the holy city and appeared to many people.' As the Old Testament believers were being transferred into heaven it would seem that some were permitted, during Jesus' visit to Mary in the garden, to rise temporarily from their graves and go into the city to testify of these wondrous tidings.

During the forty days that followed Jesus appeared many times in Jerusalem and then, with all the disciples watching, he went up out of their sight and into heaven. 'He was taken up before their very eyes, and a cloud hid him from their sight' (Acts 1.9), and the two men dressed in white told them that 'this same Jesus, who has been taken away from you into heaven will come back in the same way you have seen him go into heaven' (Acts 1.11).

To bring these things clearly into focus, let us remember that they all happened to the *man* Jesus Christ. Jesus had to remind the disciples of this when he appeared to them after his resurrection because they thought they were seeing a ghost. 'Jesus said to them, "Why are you troubled, and why do doubts rise in your minds? Look at my hands and my feet. It is I myself! Touch me and see; a ghost does not have flesh and bones, as you see I have."' And later, '"Do you have anything to eat?" They gave him a piece of broiled fish, and he took it and ate it in their presence' (Luke 24.38 and 39; and 42 and 43).

We must never forget that it was a man that was born; a man that died; a man that rose from the dead and a man who is now seated at the right hand of God the Father. The glorified man, Jesus Christ, is now head over all of God's creation. A man who is like all of us is seated in heaven and has been there for two thousand years. He is our representative and the full revelation of what we will be like.

The first-fruit on a tree is the first fully ripe fruit and it shows what the rest of the harvest will be like.

In the same way Jesus, risen and glorified, is an archetype of those who have believed in him. That is why the New Testament tells us, 'Set your hearts on things above, where Christ is seated at the right hand of God. Set your minds on things above, not on earthly things . . . When Christ, who is your life, appears, then you will appear with him in glory' (Col.3.1,2 and 4).

The New Testament gives a clear witness that he is now in heaven. The first martyr, Stephen, horrified his listeners when he looked up and exclaimed: 'I see heaven open and the Son of Man standing at the right hand of God' (Acts 7,56). Paul testifies of it in many places and in 1 Timothy 3.16 he outlines the course of Jesus' life: 'He appeared in a body, was vindicated by the Spirit, was seen by angels, was preached among the nations, was believed on in the world, was taken up in glory.' His ascension is said to be 'in glory' because it marked the end of Jesus' earthly humiliation and limitation and the beginning of his exaltation. In the book of Revelation, John describes Jesus as he now appears in glory: 'His head and hair were white like wool, as white as snow, and his eyes were like blazing fire. His feet were like bronze glowing in a furnace, and his voice was like the sound of rushing waters. His face was like the sun shining in all its brilliance' (Revelation 1.14–16).

His position in heaven is one of honour, authority and universal lordship, and from there he will return to manifest his authority and glory on the earth (Rev. 19.11–16).

'Therefore God exalted him to the highest place and gave him the name that is above every name, that at the name of Jesus every knee should bow, in heaven and on earth and under the earth, and every tongue confess that Jesus Christ is Lord to the glory of God the Father' (Phil. 2.9–11).

When God gave Moses exact instructions concerning the building of the tabernacle and the priestly service, he wanted them both to show pictorially the separation between God and man. Hence the tabernacle had two parts to it: one was called the Holy Place and could be entered by the priests; the other was called the Holiest of Holies and here the Shekinah – God's presence – was manifested. The two were separated by a veil or curtain, as opposite.

The only time the Holiest of Holies was entered was on the Day of Atonement, when the high priest, without his beautiful garments but dressed just in linen clothes, went in alone to make an atonement for the sins of the nation. Because he was imperfect he had first to sprinkle the blood of a bullock for his own sins and only then could the blood of a goat be poured out for the nation.

Because the sacrifice was imperfect, the high priest could never sit down, for his job was never done. The same ceremony had to be repeated every year because the sin problem was never completely solved.

When Jesus died, the veil in the Temple, which signified the same as that of the tabernacle, was torn in two to show that God and man were reconciled at last. At his ascension Jesus, the perfect high priest, entered into heaven and was able to sit down because God had accepted him and the infinite sacrifice of his own blood once and for all.

'Nor did he enter heaven to offer himself again and again, the way the high priest enters the Most Holy Place every year with blood that is not his own . . . Christ was sacrificed once to take away the sins of many people' (Hebrews 9.25 and 28).

'But when this priest had offered for all time one sacrifice for sins, he sat down at the right hand of God . . . because by one sacrifice he has made perfect for ever those who are being made holy' (Hebrews 10.12 and 14).

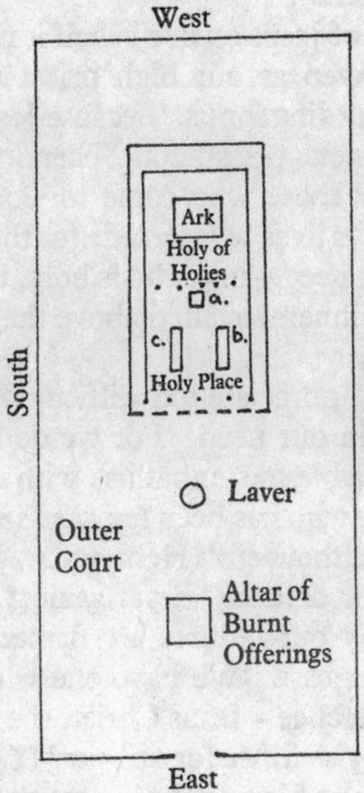

a. Altar of Incense.
b. Table of Shewbread.
c. Candlestick.

He who was humbled and who 'trod the winepress alone' still sits in heaven and his sacrifice still avails for us.

His ascension meant that Jesus could send the Holy Spirit as he had promised in John 16.7 and the Holy Spirit here is not only convicting the world of sin (John 16.8) but also revealing and manifesting Jesus and all of his work in believers' lives. The Holy Spirit indwells all who are believers (Romans 8.9) and is constantly leading us into all truth and changing us from glory to glory (2 Cor. 3.18), Because of the Holy Spirit's work, the Lord Jesus is not far away, but within us, and he will never leave nor forsake us. (Matthew 28.20).

The ministry of Jesus on our behalf is many-sided: –

1) He is in heaven as our high priest and there he is constantly interceding for us. 'Because Jesus lives forever, he has a permanent priesthood. Therefore he is able to save completely those who come to God through him, because he always lives to intercede for them. Such a high priest meets our need – one who is holy, blameless, pure, set apart from sinners, exalted above the heavens' (Hebrews 7.24 – 26).

He is able to appreciate our difficulties and so able to provide for us in our need. 'For we do not have a high priest who is unable to sympathise with our weaknesses, but we have one who has been tempted in every way, just as we are – yet without sin' (Hebrews 4.15).

2) He acts as our defence lawyer against our accuser the devil. Every day our failures are named in heaven but Jesus pleads our case. 'We have one who speaks to the Father in our defence – Jesus Christ, the Righteous One. He is the atoning sacrifice for our sins' (1 John 2.1 and 2).

3) He is preparing a place for us in heaven (John 14.3), and his presence there assures us that we will follow.

4) He answers the prayers that we pray in his name. 'And I will do whatever you ask me in my name, so that the Son may bring glory to the Father. You may ask me for

anything in my name and I will do it' (John 14.13).
5) He is the head of the Church and the one who produces growth in it (Col. 1.18, and Eph. 4.15 and 16).

As we progress in our revelation of his victory in us, we will see more and more the vital importance of the Ascension. He has gone before us into the realms of glory, and because he has been accepted, so will we be. As we now go on to examine the brilliant way in which God has applied the finished work of Christ to us who believe, we need to pray for ourselves the prayer which Paul prayed for the members of the Church: –

'I keep asking that the God of our Lord Jesus Christ, the glorious Father, may give you the spirit of wisdom and revelation, so that you may know him better. I pray also that the eyes of your heart may be enlightened in order that you may know the hope to which he has called you, the riches of his glorious inheritance in the saints, and his incomparably great power for us who believe. That power is like the working of his mighty strength, which he exerted in Christ when he raised him from the dead and seated him at his right hand in heavenly realms . . . (Eph. 1.17–20).

6: The church: God's secret weapon

The glorious truths which we have studied so far are the essential principles of our faith, and we neglect them at our peril. Our victory and our life in Christ are based on his own person and the work which he completed and any attempt to by-pass it or gloss over it will lead rapidly to an uncertain footing and certain disaster. Paul was preoccupied in his writing with 'Christ and him crucified' (1 Cor. 2.2), with his resurrection and his ascension, for he knew that God's people, who have so often perished through lack of knowledge and understanding, must know the truth if they are to be free. 'The devil prowls around like a roaring lion looking for someone to devour' and our only hope is to 'resist him, standing firm in the faith' (1 Peter 5.8 and 9).

Today the church is filled with believers who have been duped by the enemy into defeat and desolation and who remain in ignorance through lack of Bible teaching and their own laziness. It is time for the sleeping giants to awaken and take their place as victors. To this end the Holy Spirit is shouting in our day, 'Wake up, O sleeper, rise from the dead, and Christ will shine on you' (Eph. 5.14).

We must beware in these days of 'itching ears' that we don't live on spiritual convenience foods which are simple to digest, but which promote neither growth nor strength. A few years ago an entymologist was assigned to the study of the development of butterflies. He had been intrigued to see the tremendous struggle that the butterfly had to free itself from its chrysalis, and thinking that this was a time-consuming phase which he could well speed up, he decided to help the emerging butterflies by cutting the end off their chrysalids with a minute circular saw. As a result the butterflies slipped out without effort, but were then unable to fly. The struggle to emerge was not the time-waster he had imagined, but rather an action designed to develop and strengthen the muscles in their wings. Some believers today prefer ease in their Christian lives to discipline and effort, but such remain spiritual babes who have to be fed 'with milk, and not with meat' (1 Cor. 3.1–2 KJV). Buoyed up by endless testimonies and quick sermonettes they achieve easy freedom, but then lack the spiritual robustness to overcome the daily difficulties of life and fail to soar into the high things of God. When all is well they blossom, but when difficulties come they panic and collapse. Their roots are too shallow because they have avoided the training in godliness which God wants of us all.

We must devote ourselves, like athletes and soldiers, to our faith, and allow God to train us so that we 'will in all things grow up into him' (Eph. 4.15). Only thus can we become mature, 'attaining to the whole measure of the fulness of Christ' (Eph. 4.13).

The Church of Jesus Christ which is in the world today and of which we are all part is 'the fulness of him who fills everything in every way.' It is not 'a lonely-hearts club', or 'gas-ring' as its devil-inspired critics maintain, but the most brilliant and devastating creation of God. It is so hateful to Satan that he wishes at all costs to neutralise it, for every member of the Church reminds him of the Cross where he was 'disarmed' and held up as 'a public spectacle' (Col. 2.15).

Despite having had the rulership of the earth handed over to him by the first Adam, Satan is now confronted by a large number of people who have been delivered from his kingdom, who belong to his Enemy and over whom he can legally exercise no permanent control. All he can hope to achieve is to put them out of action temporarily by his lies and cunning. Fortunately, 'we are not ignorant of his devices' (2 Cor. 2.11 KJV). God's plan was so brilliant and unexpected that it has left Satan stunned, for in the Church even the weakest, most ignorant and pathetic of believers receives victory which is completely fool- and devil-proof.

God's plan was not revealed until it was outlined by Paul as he received it from the Lord himself. It had been mentioned by Jesus, but not in detail and it was unknown to the Old Testament prophets. Hence it never appeared in the Old Testament Scriptures and was, therefore, a complete mystery to Satan himself. Paul is very clear about this: 'Surely you have heard about the administration of God's grace that was given to me for you, that is, the mystery made known to me by revelation . . . which was not made known to men in other generations as it has now been revealed by the Spirit to God's holy apostles and prophets. This mystery is that through the gospel the Gentiles are heirs together with Israel, members together of one body and sharers together in the promise in Christ Jesus (Eph. 3.2–6). 'Although I am less than the least of all God's people, this grace was given me: to preach to the Gentiles the unsearchable riches in Christ, and to make plain to everyone the administration of this mystery, which for ages past was kept hidden in God, who created all things' (Eph. 3.8–9).

The perspective of the Old Testament prophets had been that which many hill-walkers have experienced, who think the summit they are aiming to reach is just ahead, but who then find a huge valley separating them from it. Diagrammatically we can show it thus: –

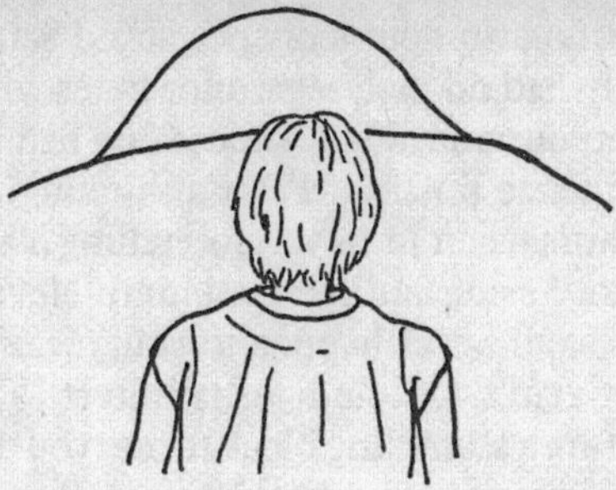

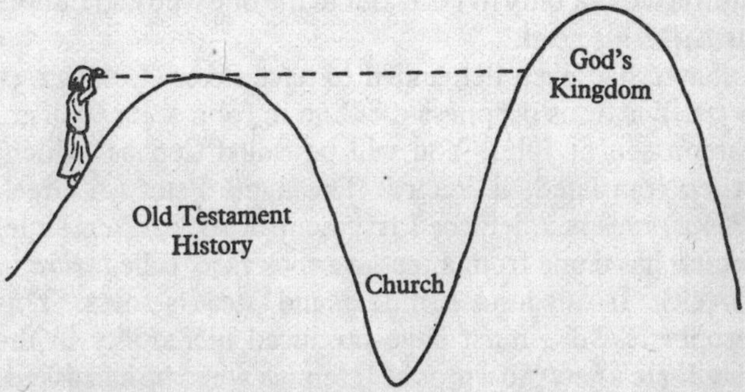

The Church of Jesus Christ and all of its power and glory were unknown. Satan had seen God's plan to establish a holy people in Israel, and had seen how their constant sinfulness and backslidings had apparently thwarted it from the beginning. He was, therefore, quite confident that even if Jesus Christ managed to defeat him, he would still have full control over the earth and its people and the ability to swing God's plan off course. When he saw the twelve disciples whom Jesus had called he was unimpressed. Mainly they were uneducated, untrained fishermen from Galilee; indeed, the only one of education and nobility seemed to be Judas Iscariot, who was firmly one of his seed.

Certain things undoubtedly perplexed Satan, however. He certainly had no high regard for Peter whom he knew to be impetuous and weak. Indeed, he had already been able to influence much of Peter's thinking. In Matthew 16.21 onwards when Jesus was foretelling his death, Peter took the Lord aside and rebuked him, 'Never, Lord!' he said, 'This shall never happen to you!' (v22). He was all too easily Satan's tool and Jesus' retort, 'Out of sight, Satan! You are a stumbling block to me; you do not have in mind the things of God, but the things of men' (v23) was addressed not only to Peter but to the one who had put the idea into his head.

Satan had even demanded to have Peter (Luke 22.31–32). Yet Jesus prophesied of him in John 1.42: 'You are Simon son of John. You will be called Cephas (which, when translated, is Peter)'. The name Peter (in Greek *Petros*) means a detached fragment of rock, often large, which has come from a massive rock face (called *petra* in Greek). It suggests firmness and steadfastness. This prophetic word must have produced incredulity in the devil. He knew the words of Jeremiah when he had asked, 'Can the Ethiopian change his skin or the leopard its spots?' (Jer. 13.23) yet here was Jesus prophesying a total change in Simon. But worse was to come. With Jesus nearing the end of his life, and on the verge of rejection by his own people, he suddenly and unexpectedly announced his future plans. Matthew 16.18 records a statement which has had the alarm bells ringing in hell ever since. Having heard Peter's confession that he was 'the Christ, the Son of the living God,' Jesus then says, 'Blessed are you Simon son of Jonah, for this was not revealed to you by man, but by my Father in heaven. And I tell you that you are Peter (*Petros*) and on this rock (*Petra*) I will build my church and the gates of Hades will not overcome it' (Matt. 16.17–18). The word *petra* is only used of Christ himself in the New Testament (in Romans 9.33; 1 Corinthians 10.4 and 1 Peter 2.8) and it is certain that he is the massive rock on which the Church is founded.[1] 1 Corinthians 3.11 is clear: 'For no-one can lay any foundation other than the one already laid, which is Jesus Christ.' Indeed, Daniel talks of him as such in Daniel 2.35 (cf Daniel 2.44). Why then is 'this rock' mentioned in the same sentence as Peter? It is because the confession Peter had made concerning Christ would be used on the day of Pentecost as the means of saving three thousand souls who would begin the church. A glance at Acts 2 will confirm that Peter's whole address is concerned with Christ.

Jesus' promise to build his church was followed by a remark which must have reverberated around Satan's headquarters, 'and the gates of hell shall not prevail against it' (Matt. 16.18 KJV). Here was something of which Satan knew nothing, yet which carried the banner of outright, unassailable victory. Satan and his angelic spy network must have been spellbound. No entry under 'Church of Jesus Christ' had ever appeared in Encyclopaedia Satanica!

Many believers have failed to understand the words of Jesus here. They have pictured a conflict in which hell is a stronghold with its gates heavily fortified and the church is an invader advancing uphill to capture it. So the prophecy is that the gates of hell will be forced open by the Church's onslaught and eventually hell's domination will be broken. Such an inverted picture can cause believers to live as if this is the case – crushed and broken by the relentless uphill struggle to capture areas of their lives dominated by Satan and his troops. Actually they have fallen prey to a deception perpetrated by the father of lies, and had they only seen the total victory which Jesus had already won against Satan and his generals at the Cross they would know that this cannot be a true picture.

In fact, the key to this passage lies in understanding what is meant by the words 'the gates'. The cities of the ancient world were protected by very large strong walls with gates set at intervals in them. Sometimes the walls were massive. For example, Babylon in Nebuchadnezzar's day had two walls, the outer one being three hundred and eleven feet tall and eighty-seven feet wide: so wide in fact that chariot races could be held on top. The entrances, therefore, consisted of two pairs of gates – one pair on the outside of the wall, and the other on the inside – to provide double protection. By closing both sets of gates they made a secure enclosed chamber in which the elders and leaders of the city used to hold council meetings to discuss plans for the future. The word 'gates', therefore, came to mean the plans or schemes of the leaders of a city. Proverbs 31.23 shows this clearly in the passage concerning a woman of noble character, 'her husband is respected at the city gate, where he takes his seat among the elders of the land.' 'The gates of hell,' therefore, meant all the satanic plans and devices which would be made in the future against the Church. Jesus, who is *omniscient*, knew every plot that would be hatched by Satan and his demons against the Church, and therefore when he prophesied that they would 'not prevail', he was speaking from certain knowledge. Understanding this changes the whole picture. The Church which Jesus was going to build would hold the top ground, it would be a 'city on a hill' (Matthew 5.14), and despite all the cunning attempts of the enemy to defeat and remove it, the Church would remain secure.

But how was God going to ensure that the disciples and all of those who believed in him would experience this victory and become more than conquerors?

As we shall see, God's amazing plan hinged upon the ministry of the Holy Spirit. Jesus said, 'It is for your good that I am going away' (John 16.7), and the truth is that without his ascension the Holy Spirit would not have come and would not, therefore, have made possible the glorious things which are now true of the Church. How often we hear believers expressing the desire to see and hear Jesus and learn at his feet. Jesus, however, said, 'blessed are those who have not seen and yet have believed' (John 20.29), and Peter, writing many years later, agrees and says, 'Though you have not seen him, you love him; and even though you do not see him now, you believe in him and are filled with an inexpressible and glorious joy' (1 Peter 1.8).

One part of the Holy Spirit's work concerns the relationship between Christ and his Church. There are many pictures of this relationship given in the New Testament; for example, the good shepherd with the sheep; the bridegroom and the bride; and the vine and the branches, but none is so glorious or far-reaching in its significance as that of the Church as the body of Christ and Jesus as the Head. It is used more than any other picture and Paul bases much of his teaching on it. The Church is seen as the very body of Jesus which Satan failed to conquer on the earth and which, therefore, has already scored victory. 'He is the head of the body, the church' (Col. 1.8).

Although it was to be several years after Jesus' resurrection and ascension that these deep truths were expounded, God gave two hints about what he had in mind at the death of Jesus. The first is simple but quite profound. When Jesus was taken to die Matthew simply records that, 'They came to a place called Golgotha (which means the Place of the Skull)' (Matthew 27.33). The skull, of course, forms the main structure of the head and it is not beyond reason to see the hand of God silently marking it out as the place where the future Head of the Church would give his life.

The second concerns the arrangement of the grave-clothes in the empty tomb. When John and Peter heard that the tomb was empty they ran to see for themselves. John, the younger man, arrived first but stopped outside. When Peter arrived he rushed straight in. 'Then Simon

Peter . . . arrived and went into the tomb. He saw the strips of linen lying there, as well as the burial cloth that had been around Jesus' head. The cloth was folded up by itself, separate from the linen' (John 20.6–7). As the body rose the grave-clothes would have collapsed where they were, and the cloth on the head would have also flattened out and be lying at the head of the grave-clothes. In fact, while the grave-clothes were lying in place as expected, the burial cloth was rolled up and in a place by itself away from the others. It is so easy to overlook such detail as unimportant but in fact here is a witness to what God had planned. Jesus would rise as the Head of the body, but leave the body on earth, in this realm of death, until the plan was complete. All believers would then constitute that body and be added to it at conversion. The Church is the body of Christ – already glorious, already victorious and now nearing the time of completion when every member will have come in. Adding believers to the body of Christ is just one of over thirty things which the Holy Spirit does to them at conversion.

This work is spoken of in 1 Corinthians 12.13, 'we are all baptised by one Spirit into one body – whether Jews or Greeks, slaves or free – and were all given the one Spirit to drink.' Irrespective of race, nationality or social status, all who believe in Christ are baptised into one body. The Holy Spirit takes each one and individually joins him to the body. The same baptism is referred to in Ephesians 4.4, 'There is one body and one Spirit – just as you were called to one hope when you were called – one Lord, one faith, one baptism, one God and Father of all, who is over all and through all and in all.'

It is usual for believers today to associate the word 'baptism' with water but in fact, the majority of the many baptisms listed in the Bible have nothing at all to do with water. The word 'baptism' certainly does mean 'to submerge or immerse' but it does not specify into what. Its exact meaning becomes clear when its use is examined. In ancient Greece, the Spartans used the word to describe one of the rituals that their warriors had to go through before going into battle. The soldiers would line up and one after another baptise their swords by plunging them into the body of a pig. As the bloodstained sword was drawn out having been baptised into blood, it was believed to be so identified with blood that it had become a successful weapon for battle. 'To baptise' therefore meant 'to identify with' and implied a change in nature.

That this is also a biblical idea can be seen from the 'baptism of Moses'. In 1 Corinthians 10.2 it is said that the generation who left Egypt with Moses 'were all baptised into Moses in the cloud and in the sea.' This simply meant that they identified themselves with Moses and went with him wherever he went. It is possible to imagine the faith and determination needed to follow Moses when we realise that at any time the towering cliffs of water on either side of the dry path through the Red Sea could have come crashing down! The planning of God in organising the forces of Pharaoh to chase the Israelites was a masterstroke and ensured the deliverance of the most fainthearted.

Their identification with Moses transformed them. While they had been west of the Red Sea in Egypt they had been enslaved, beaten down and under Pharaoh's rod; afterwards to the east they were rich, free and a nation in their own right.

In a similar way when the Holy Spirit baptised us into Christ we became fully identified with him and changed. Having been born in the first Adam, and into his slavery and failure, we were then taken out and placed into the Last Adam and hence into all that he had achieved. This is what Satan had never reckoned on, that believers who came after Jesus would be devil-proof because their lives would be 'hidden with Christ in God' (Col. 3.3). They wouldn't fight for victory by themselves (which would be doomed to failure), but they would come into victory in the Lord Jesus Christ. Being more than a conqueror is just that – someone else wins the battle and hands it to you. He who has 'trodden the wine-press alone' (Isaiah 63.3) has passed on to us the results of all his labours. In Revelation 19, which pictures the return of Jesus Christ to the earth, it is very significant that he alone wears 'a robe dipped in blood' while the army which follows is dressed in 'fine linen, white and clean' (v13 and 14).

Believers now appropriate the full fruit of Christ's work by their baptism into the body of Christ. As a people 'in Christ' they should, therefore, be walking around in all he achieved. Instead of the body of Christ being limited to one area as it was when Jesus walked on the earth, it is now universal and able to reach all nations on the face of the earth. Jesus is now manifested through his body in the world – he speaks, teaches, delivers, heals and reveals his glory through us. Our very bodies are 'the temples of the Holy Spirit' (1 Cor. 6.19), and whereas in the past people went to the temple, now the temple comes to them. What a change would occur in our lives and in our witness if we received a revelation of who we really are now we are in Christ!

An elderly friend of mine in London had this revelation to the extent that she believed that just to touch a person would allow the Holy Spirit to begin moving. On one occasion she travelled well beyond her station on the Underground in London just so that she could accidentally bump into a young teenager who sat opposite her and was in obvious need. Such simple faith is what God is looking for and I believe that in heaven it is more than likely that she will meet that young man. God can do much more than we imagine with simple acts of faith, and does not always need dramatic, well-organised gestures. D. L. Moody, for example, was saved by reading a tract handed to him in a chemist's shop, and then went on to lead thousands to the Lord.

The Church is indeed 'the fulness of him who fills everything in every way' (Eph. 1.23), and as we move forward we must see the truth about our position. Through no merit of our own we have been invested with all the blessings Jesus gained. Our mission is to be 'ambassadors for Christ' (2 Cor. 5.20 KJV), showing him forth by speaking his words and performing his actions.

It is essential that we examine our identification with Christ in a little more detail. In John 14.8 Philip asked Jesus if he could see the Father: 'Lord, show us the Father and that will be enough for us.' Jesus' reply is very significant. 'Don't you know me, Philip, even after I have been among you such a long time? Anyone who has seen me has seen the Father. How can you say, "Show us the Father?" Don't you believe that I am in the Father, and that the Father is in me? The words I say to you are not just my own. Rather, it is the Father, living in me, who is doing his work. Believe me when I say that I am in the Father and the Father is in me' (John 14. 9–11)., Jesus is saying that he and the Father were so identified, so inseparable that if you had seen and heard one, you had seen and heard the other. Indeed, Paul says that Christ is 'the image of the invisible God' (Col. 1.15). The phrase which expresses this total oneness is, 'I am in the Father, and the Father in me'.

Jesus then goes on to say that at some time in the future believers would be similarly identified with him, and in doing so he uses the same grammatical construction. In John 14.20 he says, 'On that day you will realise that I am in my Father, and you are in me, and I am in you.' Believers and their Lord would be inseparable, or as John says, 'as he is, so are we in this world' (1 John 4.17 KJV).

Many have tried to represent this relationship pictorially. A sponge submerged in the ocean or a red-hot poker in the fire are two which are often used. In one the sea is in the sponge and the sponge is in the sea; in the other, the poker is in the fire and the fire is in the poker. But the truth is so profound that without the Holy Spirit to help us we cannot understand it at all. Both parts of the relationship are important – 'you . . . in me,' and 'I in you'.

As our subject develops we will see many of the benefits which are ours because of the first of these relationships, i.e. that we are in Christ. Paul uses the words 'in Christ' no fewer than one hundred and sixty-four times, together with 'in the beloved,' 'by him', 'through him' and 'with him' which expresses the same truth. He shows that most of the benefits which are ours come directly from our position in Christ. Because we are in him, all that he achieved is automatically ours and his history, past, present and future is our history. Because of the miraculous work of the Holy Spirit we can accurately claim that we died with Christ, were buried with him, made alive with him, and that we are now seated with him in heaven itself. Satan failed to stop Jesus' success and victory and is totally unable to reverse it now. Hence our inheritance in Christ has transformed every part of our lives and our standing in the world. We so often take into account the effects of being born in Adam, but rarely give enough emphasis to the vast changes wrought in us when we were placed in Christ. The new birth has enabled us to throw off the yoke of bondage we inherited. It is true that we were 'dead in transgressions and sins' and that we actively 'followed the ways of this world', allowing 'the spirit who is now at work in those who are disobedient' (Eph. 2.1–2) to dominate our lives, but the greater truth is that 'anyone who is in Christ is a new creation; the old has gone, the new has come!' (2 Cor. 5.17). That is the truth we must now reckon and apply in our own lives.

The second half of the relationship, 'I in you,' is also of vital importance to us. How glorious is the truth that

Christ is in us. What was impossible before Jesus' ascension has now been made possible by the presence of the Holy Spirit whom Jesus sent from the Father, whose purpose is to reveal Christ in all of his fulness in us.

'When he, the Spirit of truth, comes, he will guide you into all truth . . . he will bring glory to me and by taking from what is mine and making it known to you' (John 16.13 and 14).

'The Holy Spirit will teach you all things' (John 14.26).

'I tell you the truth, anyone who has faith in me will do what I have been doing. He will do even greater things than these, because I am going to the Father' (John 14.12).

All over the world and in every nation the Holy Spirit is brooding and convicting unbelievers of sin, righteousness and judgment. When they believe, the Holy Spirit makes them 'alive' (John 6.63) to God, makes them new creations and 'sets the captives free,' (2 Cor. 3.17). To the Father they have become 'a people for himself', in whom he can reveal his Son. Paul in Galatians 1.15 recalls the day of his conversion with the words, 'But when God, who set me apart from birth and called me by his grace, was pleased to reveal his Son *in* me.' This is the amazing truth – he is in me!

The story is told of a minister walking by the sea who stopped to watch a boy digging a big hole. When asked what the hole was for, the boy told him that he wanted to empty the sea into it. Smiling to himself at the little boy's simplicity he walked on, until suddenly he realised an amazing truth. He had smiled at the suggestion that the sea could be fitted into a hole on the beach, and yet the Lord himself, the One who had made the sea in the first place, now dwelt in his body! 'If anyone acknowledges that Jesus is the Son of God, God lives in him and he in God' (1 John 4.15).

There are now three categories of people on this earth – Jews, Gentiles and the Church of Jesus Christ. As believers we, the Church, are citizens of the commonwealth of heaven (Phil. 3.20); we live in this fallen world and yet spread the sweet fragrance of Jesus everywhere we go. To Satan it reeks of his defeat, yet there is nothing he can do because our God 'always leads us in triumphal procession in Christ' (2 Cor. 2.14).

The Church, God's secret weapon, stands opposed to Satan and all of his work and through Jesus we have victory over him. What a brilliant plan – Jesus would defeat the devil and overcome sin and the world, and then send the Holy Spirit to make us members of that victorious body. Jesus Christ 'has become for us wisdom, righteousness, holiness and redemption' (1 Cor. 1.30).

It is with good reason that the New Testament says not that 'He gives us the battle through our Lord Jesus Christ,' but, 'Thanks be to God! He gives us *the victory* through our Lord Jesus Christ' (1 Cor. 15.57).

7: The devil under our feet

One of the things that shocked me when I was first saved was the fact that I still had times of depression and of generally feeling low. When I look at diaries from my early Christian years it seems as if half my life at that time was spent in the depths of despair. At first I sought help from some of the local Christians but after being told that we all had at least one 'cross to bear' and that depression was probably mine, I decided that I'd have to learn to live with it. I must admit that I often felt that I had been told lies about Christianity because the promise of love, peace and joy of which I had heard before my conversion had now been replaced with talk of immovable burdens and crosses. Apparently, I was expected *by God* to be suicidal for much of my life and I would have to adjust to it.

What joy it gives me to recall the day when I heard about Jesus' words, 'My yoke is easy and my burden is light' (Matt. 11.30). While out shopping I met a fine Christian whom I had hitherto seen only from a distance. Although usually the question 'How are you?' is no more than a pleasantry, when he asked me I felt he genuinely wanted to know. As a result I admitted frankly that I felt 'down' and a bit depressed. It was more the look of disbelief and incredulity which passed over his face than his words which began to convince me that something might be wrong. 'Depressed?' he said, 'but you're a born-again child of God!' He then told me not to put up with that but to resist the devil according to the promise of James 4.7.

When I got back and read 'Resist the devil and he will flee from you' I began to see for the first time that the devil had been behind much of what was happening to me, and that I had never tried to resist him in any way. I had settled into accepting that my depression, my feelings of inferiority, of being unloved and worse, unlovable, were natural and, like the law of the Medes and Persians, unchangeable. I had passively succumbed. That day marked the beginning of a major change in my life and the start of my path into freedom. I began to study what the Bible had to say about my rights as a believer. Jesus had said, 'You will know the truth, and the truth will set you free' (John 8.32), but I didn't know what the truth about Jesus' work was or what it meant in regard to my own life.

The way out of the quagmire in which I found myself eventually came through two verses in Hebrews. Being a fearful person I had begun to study what the Bible said about fear and as I went on I became engrossed with the positive aspects of fear rather than the negative. In fact, I found that believers were told to fear certain things. Obviously 'the fear of the Lord which is the beginning of wisdom' (Psalm 111.10) occupied me for some time, but then I was struck by Hebrews 4.1, 'Therefore let us fear lest, while a promise remains of entering his rest, anyone of you should seem to have come short of it' (NASV). I remembered hearing someone say that there were three hundred and sixty-five promises in the Bible – one for every day – but I knew very few and certainly wasn't in his rest. As I read this verse, therefore, I realised I had been too passive and relaxed about my whole faith. Then in Hebrews 11.33 I read of the Old Testament men of faith, that they had '*gained what was promised*; . . . shut the mouths of lions, quenched the fury of the flames . . . whose weakness was turned to strength . . . who became powerful in battle and routed foreign armies.' It seemed to me that if they had achieved these things by faith while under the Old Covenant, greater things were possible for us. As 'faith cometh by hearing, and hearing by the word of God' (Romans 10.17 KJV), I realised that my first task was to get to know what the word of God promised.

Over the next few weeks I collected verses from all over the Bible and began writing them out on large sheets of paper which I stuck on the wall of my room. I set myself the task of taking this godly medicine three times daily. Morning, midday and evening I read them all aloud.

'Cast all your anxiety on him because he cares for you' (1 Peter 5.7).

'We know that in all things God works for the good of those who love him, who have been called according to his purpose' (Romans 8.28).

'Cast your cares on the Lord and he will sustain you; he will never let the righteous fall' (Psalm 55.22).

'So do not fear, for I am with you; do not be dismayed, for I am your God. I will strengthen you and help you; I will uphold you with my righteous right hand' (Isaiah 41.10).

These and many others became my daily diet. I wrote them on cards and carried them with me so that they would always be at hand. Soon I knew them and began applying them. Gradually I was 'transformed by the renewing of my mind' (Romans 12.2 KJV) and began to see what Christ had done for me, what his thoughts were towards me, and what my privileges were as a Christian. I learned that in Christ there was no condemnation for me (Romans 8.1); that I was a new creature (2 Cor. 5.17); that I was a member of his body (Eph. 5.30); a partaker of the divine nature (2 Peter 1.4); a sharer in his righteousness (2 Cor. 5.21) and that I had eternal life (1 John 5.11). His destiny was now mine (1 Thess. 4.17); I was a joint-heir with Christ (Romans 8.17); I was a child of God (1 John 3.1); predestined to be like him (Romans 8.29); I was called, justified and glorified (Romans 8.29–30), a king and a priest (1 Peter 2.9) and now 'more than a conqueror' (Romans 8.37). All these things and many more.

It was the beginning of freedom. After just a few years of this training, during which my depression declined and finally disappeared, many other areas of my life which had been carnal also became 'captive unto Christ' (2 Cor. 10.5). Of course this is a continuous process, but knowing what our position is legally is the key.

Romans 5.3–5 and 1 Peter 1.6–7 show that believers are not immune from times of trouble and pressure, but what God promises is that in all of them he will turn the tables on Satan so that we will end up more glorious than when we started. Jesus said 'In this world you will have trouble. But take heart! I have overcome the world' (John 16.33).

Being a conqueror means taking your troops and winning the battle. Being more than a conqueror means being given the victory and spoil by the conqueror or alternatively ending a battle with more troops and generally stronger than at the beginning. Here is the truth about us – God's victory is so great that in every situation, no matter what occurs, the enemy is left feeling sorry that he ever began attacking you in the first place. An ear of wheat is blown onto the ground and trampled into the mud, and as a result brings forth a ten-fold increase. Romans 8.28 is another way of expressing it – 'we know that in all things God works for the good of those who love him.' It doesn't say all things are good, but it does promise that all will work to the good.

The first two words 'we know' are vital however. If only believers did know this then Satan would not be allowed to get away with things to which he is not legally entitled. While we must acknowledge that we will experience pressure in this world, it is my firm belief that most believers experience more than is necessary. Because they don't know their legal rights they are worn out by the enemy. How can we resist if we aren't clear about our true authority? While visiting Hungary a few years ago I found myself confronted by a policeman who was shouting angrily at me for crossing a road without permission. As a result he had stopped all traffic in that busy Budapest boulevard and it remained at a standstill for several minutes. Because he knew his authority, he had not hesitated to use it. Unless we do likewise the devil will continually cause us to be at a disadvantage, duping us into constant defeat. In a public art gallery in the north of England there was a painting which showed a man playing chess with the devil.[1] On the devil's face was a smile of triumph and he was obviously impatiently awaiting the man's next move, so that he in his turn could achieve 'checkmate'. For years it testified of the artist's belief that in life man was certain to lose.

But one day a chess expert studied the painting and discovered that unbeknown to the artist, he had so arranged the pieces that in the next move, the man could checkmate the devil. The same is true of us in our Christian lives.

What then is our legal position in regard to Satan? We now have all the information we need to answer that question.

When God created life he created it according to a pattern with a distinct order in it. Psalm 8.4 informs us of that order. 'What is man that you are mindful of him, the son of man that you care for him? You made him a little lower than the heavenly beings and crowned him with glory and honour.' This is quoted in the book of Hebrews where the 'heavenly beings' are specified as 'angels' (Heb. 2.6–8). It begins with the smallness of man. Compared to all in the heavens – God himself, the angelic beings and the stars of the universe – man is an exceedingly small part of the creation. He is weak, frail and insignificant when considered beside such power and glory. Yet, when he was created, God created him in his own image, thereby giving him a dignity and standing only a little way below that of himself and the angels who surround him. The Hebrew of

Psalm 8 is literally translated 'a little lower than God'[2] (ELOHIM) while Hebrews 2.7[3] has angels (ANGELOS). God and all the angels of the original creation are represented here. So God and the angels are highest in order, with man just below them. But man has been made king and lord over the rest of the created realm i.e. animals and plants.

We can draw this order: –

GOD
ANGELS, including Satan
MAN
ANIMALS

Even with these categories there is a hierarchy which has to be recognised and respected. Believers are told to obey those in authority over them. Romans 13.1 is clear, 'Everyone must submit himself to the governing authorities, for there is no authority except that which God has established.' In Jude 8 those who rejected authority are described as 'these dreamers' who 'pollute their own bodies, reject authority and slander celestial beings.'

Even though king Saul was grossly out of fellowship with God, David never tried to overthrow him or treat him with anything but respect. He knew that he ranked below him in authority until the day God would choose to remove him. In the angelic realm too there is a hierarchy. Satan is the highest-ranking angel, with the archangels including Gabriel and Michael below him and the others below them. Two of the ranks in Satan's forces are given in Ephesians 6.12 where they are called 'rulers' (*arche*) and 'authorities' (*exzousia*). The word *arche*, which also means 'beginning' or first', was the title held by the highest officials in a city and the 'five-star' generals in the army. These are the demons who receive direct orders from Satan himself. The 'authorities' rank below them and include all the other officer ranks who control the main body of demons.

The holy angels and fallen angels all know which position they hold and carefully avoid stepping over the boundaries. This is the reason we are told in Jude 9 that 'even the archangel Michael, when he was disputing with the devil about the body of Moses, did not dare to bring a slanderous accusation against him, but said, "The Lord rebuke you!"' It would have been quite wrong for a lesser personage to rebuke a greater, so instead he calls on one higher than Satan, namely 'the Lord' himself.

What we must now understand is that the ascension of Jesus Christ and our baptism into him have changed the order. After Jesus Christ died in his humanity he rose and ascended. Ephesians 1.20–22 is very clear, that after God had raised Jesus from the dead he 'seated him at his right hand in the heavenly realms, *far above* all rule and authority, power and dominion, and every title that can be given, not only in the present age but also in the one to come. And God placed all things under his feet and appointed him to be head over everything. . . .' The glorified man is now at the summit of creation and is seated in heaven, having been completely accepted by God.

The order therefore is now: –

GOD
JESUS CHRIST the man
ANGELS, including Satan
MAN
ANIMALS

Because of Jesus' ascension the devil and the other angels are firmly below him and truly under his feet.

Once ascended, Jesus sent forth the Holy Spirit who then baptised all believers into Christ. Where he is, therefore, so are we, and Ephesians 2.6 states the results of this by saying, 'And God raised *us* up with Christ and seated us with him in the heavenly realms in Christ Jesus.'

The amazing truth is now quite clear; because of our position in Christ all believers now rank higher than the angelic realm.

The order which applies today, therefore, is: –

GOD
JESUS CHRIST the man, head of the church
BELIEVERS, the body of Christ
ANGELS, including Satan
UNBELIEVERS
ANIMALS

As a result, believers are now officially and legally ranked higher than all the angels including Satan. This truth is so dynamic and far-reaching in its implications that Satan has tried to keep it hidden from believers – it would be too devastating for him if all believers came into a revelation of the rank they really have now that they are risen with Christ. The truth is that *the Devil is now under our feet*.

This does not mean that he will not attempt to rebel against this ranking. His initial sin, as we have seen, was to rebel against God and reject his authority, so he will certainly be true to form with us. But once we know the truth we can stand firm and he will eventually have no option but to flee. As a defeated foe, Satan is now ranked below us in authority and therefore has no right to bind any believer.

Of Jesus it is said that he 'shared in their humanity so that by his death he might destroy him who holds the power of death – that is the devil' (Hebrews 2.14). 'And having disarmed the powers and authorities he made a public spectacle of them, triumphing over them by the cross' (Col. 2.15).

In trying to conquer Jesus Christ when he was on the earth Satan exhausted his arsenal of weapons. The triumph of Jesus has proved that none of these weapons were of any effect and so Satan is now disarmed. This is the truth about him, and the truth about us is that we have been given authority over the angelic realm in him.

'Are not *all* angels (elect and fallen) ministering spirits sent to serve those who will inherit salvation' (Hebrews 1.14). This important verse is the key to the revelation that all angels can benefit us, and in the next chapter we will see that even demons can have the tables turned on them so that their actions eventually aid the believers they sought to destroy. Indeed, we can expect this as one of the benefits of being 'more than conquerors.'

'I have given you authority to trample on snakes and scorpions, and to overcome *all* the power of the enemy; nothing will harm you' (Luke 10.19).

'And these signs will accompany those who believe: In my name they will drive out demons' (Mark 16.17).

When you speak in someone's name you are speaking on their behalf. Lawyers act in our name in court and speak for us. So we, as the body of Christ, speak in the name of Jesus. When we discern Satan's activity or demonic oppression we must resist firmly in the name of Jesus. The early church exercised this authority. Acts 5.16 says, 'There came also a multitude out of the cities round about unto Jerusalem, bringing sick folks, and them which were vexed with unclean spirits: and they were healed every one' (KJV). The word 'vex' is from a Greek work which means 'to obsess, to harass, to mob or to riot' and it refers to the times when a demon or group of demons attacks or disturbs a person. We have power to stop it in Jesus' name.

The devil will try and stop us realising this authority. Recently I read a book by someone who was trying to instruct believers about deliverance. He said that it was never right to say '*I* rebuke you, Satan' and then he quoted Jude 9 where, as we have seen, the archangel Michael does not presume to rebuke Satan but said, 'The Lord rebuke you.' The author was very seriously wrong. Michael couldn't rebuke Satan because he was below him in rank, but every believer is above Satan and his angels in authority. It is, therefore, imperative for us to say, '*I* rebuke you, Satan,' and if we do not, but repeat Michael's words we are acting in unbelief and giving Satan power which he does not legally have.

Furthermore we have authority to use the blood of Jesus. Revelation 12.11 says, 'They overcame him by the blood of the Lamb and by the word of their testimony.' In our present days of apostacy many view the whole concept of blood as primitive and barbaric and there is even a move afoot to remove all references to the blood from hymns. Barbaric it may seem but God declares clearly that 'without shedding of blood there is no remission' (Hebrews 9.22 KJV). Sin is a reality and so are its effects – but remove the blood and sin is left untouched. Leviticus 17.11 tells us that 'the life is in the blood.' The only thing that overcomes the death produced by sin is life and the only thing that has life in it is the blood. In 1 John 1.7 we are told that 'if we walk in the light, as he is in the light, we have fellowship with one another, and the blood of Jesus, his Son, purifies us from every sin.' The Greek word translated 'purifies' is in the present tense which is a continuous tense and therefore this passage can be translated, 'And the blood of Jesus his Son keeps continually cleansing us from every sin.' That blood has never lost its power and is still effective today.

The blood speaks to Satan of Jesus' complete victory and causes him to shrink back in horror. There is peace in my own home and upon my life and that of my wife and children because we are diligent in ensuring that the blood of Jesus Christ is claimed for our household several times a day. At the time of the Exodus the generation of Jews whom God wanted to leave Egypt were told to kill a lamb without blemish, collect its blood and daub it onto the lintel and door-posts so that the angel of death would pass over. It would have been no use for them to have left the blood in the bowl – it became effective as it was used. So it must be with us. We are blood-bought believers, and that blood is available for us to use. To oppose Satan in Jesus' name and to claim the power of the blood of Christ is so powerful that demons do not stay around to contest it.

The word of our testimony is also powerful. To remind Satan of who we are in Christ prevents his deception and allows us to have a sure footing to resist him. 'We are children of God' (1 John 3.2); 'I am more than a conqueror' (Romans 8.37); 'It is no longer I who live, but Christ who lives in me' (Gal. 2.20). Formidable indeed is the man who stands in the revelation of who he is and claims the full protection which Jesus has provided. 'Be strong in the Lord and in *his* mighty power' (Eph. 6.10).

Let me add here that we as believers should never be flippant or blasé about our authority: it is vital that we always realise just how stunning God made our adversary and with what a high position God invested him. As any one in authority knows, it is important to have a healthy respect for those of lower rank. But we can do this without compromising our own position in any way. I have heard it said that we should laugh at the devil for it is the thing he hates most. I cannot subscribe to that view for he is a cunning enemy and all too often while believers are engaged in laughing at him, they are being outflanked. 1 Peter 5.8 says, 'Be self-controlled and alert. Your enemy the devil prowls around like a roaring lion looking for someone to devour.' Even though man has authority over the animals in the world and officially they are under him, a lack of vigilance and due respect for wild animals will end in a man being eaten for breakfast.

Nevertheless our authority is God-given and with soberness and with a revelation of the truth it can be used effectively to stop Satan's deception and attacks. It is no longer necessary for us to be kicked around and oppressed Let us therefore, both male and female believers, appropriate our legal entitlements. We have been raised with Christ 'far above all principalities and powers' and we all must be prepared to stand in the authority which we have in Christ and to oppose Satan and his work in the name of Jesus.

Romans 16.19 and 20 declares the proper balance when it says, 'I want you to be wise about what is good and innocent about what is evil. The God of peace will soon crush Satan under *your* feet.' Many believers become obsessed with the devil and spend more time thinking about him and his demons than about Christ and his victory. In doing so they are actually glorifying the devil. We are not told to be wise about evil, but about what is good. To know our enemy and his strategy is important but let us rather concentrate on the Lord's victory over him and on what we have and who we are in Christ.

To be preoccupied with Christ, and to be constantly thrilled and excited about his work for us and in us, is the way of victory. Then we are not so much resisting the enemy as living beyond his reach. Demons are like sensitive house plants; they only flourish where the climate suits them. If in our lives, relationships and homes we live selflessly for God, then demons will soon be uprooted and go away to search for cooler climes.

The church of Jesus Christ has such power and authority invested in it that Satan cannot prosper against it. Our risen Saviour who is 'far above' all authority and rule, under whose feet all has been placed, has been appointed 'to be head over everything for the church, which is his body, the fulness of him who fills everything in every way' (Eph. 1.22 and 23). 'Since, then, you have been raised with Christ, set your hearts on things above, where Christ is seated at the right hand of God. Set your minds on things above, *not* on earthly things' (Col. 3.1 and 2).

During my early years, in which I learned many of these things, I found such success in my prayers for myself and others that I became constantly occupied with the devil, demons and people in bondage. At first I rejoiced greatly in all that the Lord was doing but soon found myself oppressed and fearful. I had spent so much time and effort on the devil, that I had lost my deep relationship with the Lord. My delight was not in the Lord but in my authority over demons. Cunningly, the devil was bringing me into bondage and was seeking to bring me into a place where I would never again be confident enough to move against him. He is a subtle enemy. This is why, when the seventy returned having seen demons submitting to them through the name of Jesus, he told them, 'rejoice not, that the spirits are subject unto you; but rather rejoice, because your names are written in heaven' (Luke 10.20 KJV).

Nevertheless we are told, 'Resist the devil, and he will flee from you' (James 4.7). In the Greek it is clear that this is a command showing that it is part of every believer's ministry to oppose him. I am so thankful for the day when I realised that I had certain rights and responsibilities as a believer, and that to be free from Satan's influence was both a right and responsibility. My problem was that he had dominated so much of my life for so long that I was used to giving in to him and obeying him. I was also slow to learn the truth about myself once I was born again and in Christ. Colossians 1.13 clearly states that God 'has rescued us from the dominion of darkness and brought us into the kingdom of the Son he loves.' We have been transferred from one kingdom into another and now that the benefits of the new kingdom are ours we don't have to put up with anything from the old régime. The revelation of this only began to open up to me when I read the words of Jesus in John 14.30, 'for the prince of this world cometh and *hath nothing in me.*' (KJV). Satan's authority is subject to God and therefore Jesus didn't call him 'king' of this world – when God's time comes Satan will be overthrown and removed. But Jesus clearly states that Satan 'hath nothing in me', and I suddenly realised that because I was now in Christ, Satan legally had nothing in me either. Yet the truth which the word of God proclaimed was being contradicted by my own experience and so I realised that Satan was overstepping his rights.

One of my major problems had been fear of people. There are two ways in which people react when they are fearful like this – they either become introverted and try to hide away in the shadows, or they become extrovert. I was one of the latter and for years I covered up my fear by being overtly outward-going. Afraid of silences, I would fill up every moment with exhausting chat. Many would have found it hard to believe that the noisy and apparently self-confident individual that they had endured for years was really frightened of them. Letters and telephone calls created such tension that I was often shaking as I opened the envelope or picked up the receiver. As a teacher I taught for two years in a classroom overlooking the visitors car-park and at least twice a week became convinced that the people parking their cars below were coming to complain about me.

How I could identify with Elijah in 1 Kings 19! Elijah had just witnessed tremendous victory over Baal on Mount Carmel when the God who answers by fire had come and burnt up not only the sacrifice but the wood, the stone, the soil and all the water in the trench as well, and yet the next day he was running away in fear! Ahab the king had told his wife Jezebel what had befallen the prophets of Baal, and Jezebel, herself the high priestess of Baal, was angry. She could easily have sent an assassin to kill Elijah, but her shrewdness told her that such a course could lose her support from many of the Jews who were trying to serve God and Baal and might even cause increased fervour for the Lord God of Israel. So she decided upon a course of action which would undermine Elijah's standing in the nation and put him to flight. She simply wrote him a letter informing him that within the next twenty-four hours she would have him killed.

Elijah was filled with the fear of this woman and ran for his life. So fearful was he in fact, that he didn't stop until he reached 'Beersheba in Judah' (v3) which was one hundred miles away from the place he began. He then walked a day's journey into the wilderness where he sat down and with the 'I wish I were dead' mentality occupying his head, asked God to take him. 'I have had enough Lord,' he said, 'Take my life; I am no better than my ancestors.' (v4). He was in the type of situation so many believers have been in – assailed by a progression of fear, despair and self-pity. Just a few days beforehand he'd been leading one of the greatest revivals Israel had seen for a long time, and now he was in the depths of despair; and all because of an empty threat from a woman he feared.

Eventually he found a cold, dark, dank cave and as it suited his mood he decided to stay there. (v9) 'And the word of the Lord came to him: "What are you doing here, Elijah?"' God is asking that today of every believer who finds himself in this state: 'What are you doing here?' We who are the redeemed of the Lord and more than conquerors have not been designed to be long-distance runners or troglodytes – we are designed to stand fast and show forth the greatness of our God. We must learn from Elijah's lesson that it isn't the dramatic gestures of our God (the powerful wind, the earthquake and the fire, v11 and 12) which will release us into freedom but hearing the 'still small voice' or 'gentle whisper' of the Holy Spirit within us day by day – teaching us the great truths of our salvation.

One day, when I was suffering the 1 Kings 19 syndrome, the Holy Spirit asked me, 'Who are you that you should be in this state?' and showed me the word in Isaiah 51.12, 'I, even I, am he who comforts you. Who are you that you fear mortal men?' Fortunately by that time I knew my standing and my rights in Jesus, so I began to resist the fear. I didn't know whether it was a messenger from Satan who was causing the fear or whether my past life had caused me to be fearful; all I knew was that I was a new creation and either way I was going to be free. I went to my room, lay on my bed and began to pray and resist the fear. For three days I went to my room in every free moment and continued to rebuke it. Suddenly, sometime on the fourth day, I began to feel the fear manifesting in my body in the form of involuntary shaking. I was thrilled – I couldn't shake myself like that, and I realised that a spirit of fear was beginning to have a rough ride in my life. I found that when I stopped praying the shaking stopped instantly and I could occupy myself with other things quite normally. Day after day I spent some time rebuking it and praying against it. The promise of James 4.7 was being fulfilled; as I resisted I was becoming free.

The final day of release was a miracle. I had decided to attend a meeting where a minister from Guernsey was due to speak. Two Christian women had invited me to go to hear this man, and being a little late we sat on three seats right at the back of the room. During the minister's opening prayer he said, 'Father, you know that I don't believe I should be speaking here tonight but that you've got someone else to minister to your people. Show us who it is Lord.' Immediately I suspected that it could be me. When he had finished praying he looked up and pointing straight at me said, 'Will you come and speak to us tonight?' Before I had time to realise what I was saying I had accepted and the miracle occurred. As I stood up I felt all fear drain from me and I walked a free man to the front of that meeting. The difference was very obvious to me and since that time I have been free from the fear that had caused me to over-compensate in my behaviour with others.

The truth is that we have been delivered, and the devil

and all of his demons are under our feet. When the devil roars at you like a lion remember that you are now in the Lion of Judah and roar back. We are blood-bought people who are destined to reign with Christ and it is here on this earth that our apprenticeship begins. What a glorious army God has made us – we must take our positions and stand against the enemy.

'Whom resist steadfast in the faith,' (1 Peter 5.9 KJV) is God's command to us all regarding the devil's assault. The word 'steadfast' was a word well-known to the Greek army. It was a word used to describe a military formation called the Macedonian phalanx which was invented by Alexander the Great. It was a brilliant device which consisted of sixty-four battalions each of two-hundred and fifty-six men (a total of 16,384 men). Each man carried a huge pike eighteen feet long with a very sharp metal tip on it. They marched sixteen men deep and the first five or six rows would hold their pikes pointing horizontally towards the front, while the rows behind held them progressively more vertically, ready to be used if necessary. In this formation they marched forward through anyone who tried to stop them. When Alexander marched through Parthia the Indians brought forward two hundred elephants to resist them. After whipping the elephants into a frenzy the Indians charged them at the Greeks only to find the elephants retreating in the face of the phalanx and trampling upon their own troops. The Macedonian phalanx was undefeated for centuries.

God's command to the church is to march forward together like the phalanx. Then we'll see the enemy fleeing before us and abandoning territory he should never have had in the first place. Ours is indeed the victory and the devil is under our feet.

8: The full armour of God

The Lord Jesus Christ is Lord and Master of the universe and his work for each one of us has provided all we need to fulfil our role as his ambassadors on the earth. He is not only the 'author' of our faith but the 'finisher' too (Heb. 12.2 KJV) and 'he who began a good work in you will carry it on to completion until the day of Christ Jesus' (Phil. 1.6). 'The one who calls you is faithful and he will do it' (1 Thess. 5.24).

The idea that we are saved by faith but then left in this world to work towards the perfection of our salvation is wrong. When we come face to face with the Lord, he and he alone will receive glory for the wonderful completeness of his work in saving and delivering us. Some speak as if when we reach heaven we'll throw our arms around the shoulders of Jesus and rejoice in the joint work; as though he had done his part and we ours, and that together we had earned our place in heaven. It is not so. Jesus said, 'freely ye have received' (Matt. 10.8) and he was very insistent that 'the spirit gives life; the flesh counts for nothing' (John 6.63). The life we live on this earth is only effective for God because of his work and the presence of the Holy Spirit in us. 'The life I live in the body, I live by faith in the Son of God, who loved me and gave himself for me' (Gal. 2.20). All we have is in Jesus and his work has provided for our every need. 'From the fulness of his grace we have all received one blessing after another' (John 1.16).

'For in him dwelleth all the fulness of the Godhead bodily. And ye are complete in him, which is the head of all principality and power' (Col. 2.9 and 10 KJV).

While he was on earth, he had total mastery and no-one was able to have power over him without his permission. When Judas Iscariot came to betray Jesus on the Mount of Olives he came with a 'detachment of soldiers and some officials from the chief priests and Pharisees. They were carrying torches, lanterns and weapons' (John 18.3). With the exception of Peter, who had suspected that there might be trouble that night and had therefore hidden a sword in his clothing, Jesus and the disciples were unarmed and after the betraying kiss some might presume that Jesus had been forced to accompany the group back to Jerusalem to face trial. To show that he wasn't forced but that he went of his own free-will, a very interesting incident is recorded.

'Jesus, knowing all that was going to happen to him, went out and asked them, "Who is it you want?" "Jesus of Nazareth," they replied. "I am he," Jesus said. When Jesus said "I am he," they drew back and fell to the ground (John 18.4–6).

The impact of this passage is lost because the translators had added the little word 'he' to the words 'I am'. In fact Jesus used the name of God, 'I am' and applied it to himself; and as he did so, for a split second, the fulness of his divinity shone forth causing the fully-armed band of men to fall powerless to the ground. Therefore when Jesus accompanied them to Jerusalem they all knew that he was coming with them because he chose to come and not because they had any power over him.

Just as Jesus had complete mastery in his life, he also had complete mastery when he died (see chapter five), and when he ascended into heaven he went with the purpose of showering us with the benefits of his completed work.

We, the Church, have been given victory because we are the body of Christ and as individual members of that body each one of us has received the fulness of blessing. It is the devil who is now seeking to rob us of our victory.

From time to time we hear talks or see articles based on various Scriptures from Revelation 2 and 3 on the subject of 'Overcomers'. In them we are subjected to various threats and warned about the consequences of not overcoming the world – that we'll not make it to heaven, or won't be in the rapture of the Church and so on. They make it sound as if the work isn't complete; as if we are still in defeat and having to complete the work through *our* own efforts. They quote the book of Revelation but conveniently overlook the former writings of its author John. Among the books of the New Testament it is interesting to note that those which were written later contain more warnings about false teachers and false brethren infiltrating the church. It is clear that the devil's counter-attack against the early church was extremely rapid, and it would seem that within sixty years there were religious, yet unregenerate people in the midst. The letters to the churches in Revelation were written to mixed congregations and they contained warnings to those not truly converted. The true believers are identified by the phrase 'those who overcome' (Rev. 2.7; Rev. 2.11; Rev. 2.17; Rev. 2.26; Rev. 3.5; Rev. 3.12; Rev. 3.21). By referring to the earlier writings of John we can more easily understand these verses. Let us see how John defined 'the overcomers' in his first epistle.[1]

'I write to you, young men, because you *have* overcome the evil one' (1 John 2.13).

'You, dear children, are from God and *have* overcome them, *because the one who is in you is greater than the one who is in the world*' (1 John 4.4).

'*For everyone born of God has overcome the world*. This is the victory that has overcome the world, even our faith' (1 John 5.4).

'*Who is it that overcomes the World? Only he who believes that Jesus is the Son of God*' (1 John 5.5).

This is an example of the Bible as its own commentary.

Revelation 2 and 3 can only be correctly understood against the background of 1 John. Here you do not find the teaching that by our own efforts we overcome the world. That is a lie of the devil designed to rob us of what we already have in Christ. By it, Satan would cause us to move in the flesh, to become legalistic and eventually to be worn out and crushed. In fact, the overcomers are not some special super-spiritual Christians, but normal Christians like you and me.

If we believe that Jesus is the Son of God we have already overcome, and are already overcomers. Not by our work but because he that is in us is greater than he that is in the world. The things promised to the overcomers in Revelation 2 and 3 are, in fact, already ours, and it will be worth our while looking at them more closely in order to see this clearly.

'To him who overcomes I will give the right to eat from the tree of life, which is in the paradise of God' (Rev. 2.7) – a promise of eternal life and health.

'He who overcomes will not be hurt at all by the second death' (Rev. 2.11). The second death is defined in Revelation 20.14 as the lake of fire, so the promise is that no believer will be cast into the lake of fire.

'To him who overcomes, I will give some of the hidden manna. I will also give him a white stone . . .' (Rev. 2.17). There were three items placed in the Ark of the Covenant which the Jews carried around: the tablets of the Law which spoke of keeping God's commandments; Aaron's rod which represented God's authority; and a dish of manna which spoke of his provision. These provided a picture of the work of Jesus Christ: he would forgive the breaking of the Law; the rebellion against God's authority, and the rejection of all he had provided. The hidden manna in the Ark also referred to God's provision for our need in every circumstance and it is promised to all believers.

The 'white stone' simply shows us that we are his elect and chosen ones. In ancient Athens, debates about the future of a city and the elections of officials were held in public and each person listening was given a white and a black stone. If a person agreed with what was being proposed or wanted to vote for a particular nominee, they simply left the white stone in the ballot box. If they disagreed, then the black stone was left. God votes for all who are born again and the white stone speaks of his election.

'To him who overcomes . . . I will give authority over the nations' (Rev. 2.26) – a promise that when Christ reigns on the earth we will rule with him.

'He who overcomes will, like them, be dressed in white. I will never erase his name from the book of life, but will acknowledge his name before my Father and his angels' (Rev. 3.5) – all believers receive the righteousness of Christ and are eternally secure in God.

'Him who overcomes I will make a pillar in the temple of my God' (Rev. 3.12) – the future heavenly city is considered as a temple and in it we believers will hold important, key positions.

'To him who overcomes, I will give the right to sit with me on my throne, just as I overcame and sat down with my Father on his throne' (Rev. 3.21) – all believers are kings and rule with his authority.

These verses contain no promise which is not made to believers in other parts of the New Testament and applied to all. From the least to the greatest of us, our confession must be that we are overcomers.

Nevertheless, while our enemy the devil and his agents are seeking to destroy us, we must be vigilant. This is why in Ephesians 6 we are told to 'put on the full armour of God'. It is important to realise that his armour is for defensive purposes only – we have no need of offensive weapons because we are already victors.

'Finally, be strong in the Lord and in his mighty power. Put on the full armour of God so that you can take your stand against the devil's schemes. For our struggle is not against flesh and blood, but against the rulers, against the authorities, against the powers of this dark world and against the spiritual forces of evil in the heavenly realms. Therefore put on the full armour of God, so that when the day of evil comes, you may be able to stand your ground, and after you have done everything, to stand' (Eph. 6.10–13).

Paul was writing this from a prison where he was chained to Roman soldiers for twenty-four hours every day. Three soldiers a day would have had the job of guarding him for eight hours each. Paul refers to these chains in Ephesians 6.20 'for which I am an ambassador in chains.' I believe that Paul would probably have used the time as an opportunity to preach to the soldiers and at times they must have wondered whether perhaps they were the real prisoners. But Paul was in a position to know all about the armour of a Roman soldier and he used it as the model for our spiritual armour. He names six pieces of equipment:-

(a) the belt
(b) the breastplate
(c) the shoes
(d) the shield
(e) the helmet and
(f) the sword.

In fact, however, the full Roman armour was much more extensive than this list. It varied, but always had offensive weapons chosen from the following: – two javelins – large and small, a spear, a lance, a club, a bow, a catapult, a sling, a dagger, and many other things. They were cleverly designed. The problem with the javelin, for example, was that once it was thrown the enemy could use it to throw back, and so the Romans had designed one which crumpled on impact so that it could not then be used against them.

The 'full armour of God', however, is totally lacking in these offensive weapons for the simple reason that our God has already won the battle and therefore we have no use for them. As those who already occupy the high places, all we have to do is to defend what is already ours. This is the message of the armour – we already have the victory, but Satan is trying to dislodge us from it and the armour is needed to enable us to stand our ground against his attacks, as seen below.

Let us therefore consider the six pieces of armour referred to in Ephesians 6 as the 'full armour of God'.

The belt.

'Stand firm then, with the belt of truth buckled around your waist,' v14. This was the basic piece of dress to which everything else was attached and it was called the Baldric. It was a broad leather belt fastened around the waist and sometimes, when heavy armour was needed, a strap which went over the shoulder was added to it. In the Christian's armour the waist-band is sufficient.

The breastplate, the scabbard for the sword and the pieces of leather which gave protection to the lower part of the body were all attached to it. The Roman soldier would attach discs of various metals onto it which told of the campaigns in which he had fought. If the belt was loose, then nothing else would hold firm and combat would be impossible.

In the Christian's armour this belt is called 'truth' and it is fundamental. We have to know what Jesus accomplished for us, what he has done to the enemy and what standing we now have with him, for if any part of this truth is insecure in our lives then our defensive garment will be less effective. This is why so much of this book has been devoted to these essentials.

Undoubtedly, the truth referred to here also means

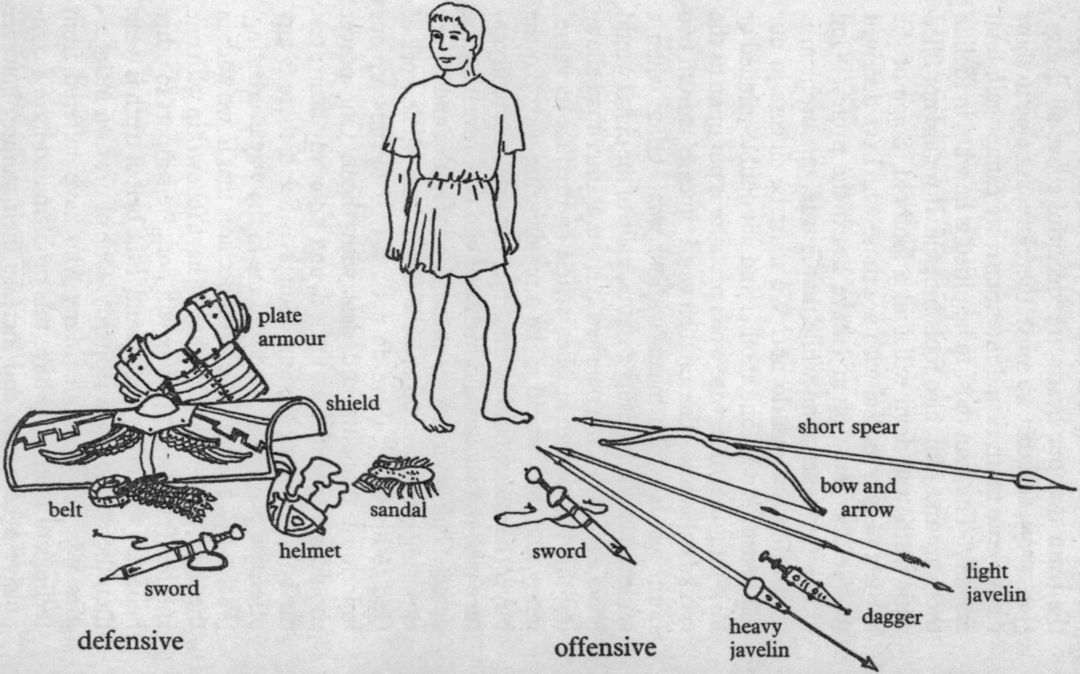
plate
armour
shield
belt
sandal
helmet
sword
defensive
short spear
bow and
arrow
sword
light
javelin
dagger
heavy
javelin
offensive

'truth in the inner parts' (Psalm 51.6). Until we face up to the truth that our hearts are 'deceitful above all things' (Jer. 17.9), and that we must, therefore, ask God to show us our true motives and intentions, we cannot gain total mastery. The man most to be pitied is he who, in fooling those around him, also fools himself. If we are not filled with truth, the devil will find a foothold. Some of the hardest people to deal with are those who have deceived themselves. How often I have heard the protest 'God knows my heart', and while that is true, our problem is very often that we do not. We must be sincere in our relationships with one another and not double-minded or fork-tongued, otherwise when pressure is put upon us the cracks will show. The English word 'sincere' is from two Latin words which mean 'without wax'. Often when a sculptor was completing a statue, a slip of the chisel would leave a scar on some polished surface. Rather than allowing this to ruin the finished article and reduce its value, many sculptors would make a repair using wax. To the buyer the fault would be invisible, but when the temperature rose the wax would melt and run out, revealing the defect. The devil can see through our façades and we are exposing ourselves, other believers and the whole work of God to his attack if we do not ask God to show up our innermost thoughts and deal with them. Our prayer should be, 'Search me, O God, and know my heart; test me and know my anxious thoughts. See if there is any offensive way in me, and lead me in the way everlasting' (Psalm 139.23–24). The word declares that if 'we walk in the light, as he is in the light, we have fellowship with one another (1 John 1.7). Wax will not give support to other believers when they need it and if the belt of truth is weak then the warrior is in jeopardy. One of my own insincerities was exaggeration. Many who have suffered from feelings of inferiority have this problem and have a compulsive need to try and increase their stature, however marginally, in every situation. I asked the Lord to tell me when I was about to exaggerate so that I could check myself. He faithfully answered my prayer and very often enabled me to make mid-sentence corrections in my conversation.

Our longing should be that like Paul we may testify that 'we have conducted ourselves in the world, and especially in our relations with you, in the holiness and sincerity that are from God' (2 Cor. 1.12).

The breastplate.

'The breastplate of righteousness in place' (v14).

The breastplate was made from metals like gold and silver, or from horn and skin reinforced with metal strips. It was anchored to the belt and gave protection to the vital organs in the upper part of the body. It was so stiff that, when taken off, it stood by itself and was often used by the soldiers as a rest to sit on. Putting it on was difficult and took much practice.

The breastplate of a Christian is said to be 'righteousness' and it refers to the imputed righteousness which we received the moment we believed in Christ. 'God made him who had no sin to be sin for us, so that in him we might become the righteousness of God' (2 Cor. 5.21). This righteousness stands by itself because it is a result of his work alone and when the devil comes to accuse us, we can be protected inside it. The Bible says that we are sanctified (made holy) in Christ the moment we believe, but also that experientally we become more holy in our daily lives as the Holy Spirit continues working in us. When at last he appears, our sanctification will be complete in our bodies. 'Everyone who has this hope in him purifies himself, just as he is pure' (1 John 3.3). His imputed righteousness enables us to stand in this world, and encourages us to seek God that he may deal with sin in our lives.

Many people find it very difficult to put on the righteousness of Christ: when they see obvious problem areas in their lives, and sins which seem so difficult to conquer, they tend to condemn themselves. 1 John 1.9 tells us to confess our sins to God and to trust in his faithfulness and justice to forgive us. This confession is an essential part of the breastplate. The church of Jesus Christ must be sanctified and we must seek God to cleanse our ways.

The shoes.

'With your feet fitted with the readiness that comes from the gospel of peace' (v15). The shoes were vitally important to a soldier for they had to provide a sure footing during the fight. If you are slipping and uncertain of your ground then your enemy has an advantage. You have to be so sure-footed that all your energy can be directed at your opponent. Through years of experience the Romans developed shoes for their army which were sandal-like but had soles half-an-inch thick, with studs underneath. The officers in the army also had leather gaiters which were wound around the foot, ankle and leg. On whatever ground they were used, they provided a firm footing. A literal translation of Ephesians 6.15 is, 'And your feet shod with the anticipation of the good news of peace' and refers to the anticipation of the certainty of Jesus' victory. Often we find ourselves in situations which seem so chaotic that we can't see the way ahead and at these times we must be certain of the eventual outcome. In the Bible this is represented by the word 'hope'. Hope has been debased in its meaning in our day. Most of us now use 'hope' as a word which expresses an uncertain outcome: we hope that it will not rain tomorrow, or hope that we've passed an examination. The word as used in the Bible is not like that – biblically, 'hope' is *the certainty* that something will occur. 'Christ in you, the hope of glory' (Col. 1.27) expresses the certainty that we will be glorified at some future date because Christ is in us. Those who 'hope in Christ' (1 Cor. 15.19) therefore have certainty in their hearts – not uncertainty.

Often in our warfare we pray for and believe for things which may take time to come, but as long as we are certain of his victory we can stand firm. This applies in many areas of our lives. During the period of two or three years in which the Lord dealt with my depression, it was the certainty that the Lord would eventually free me totally which enabled me to remain steadfast. As the writer to the Hebrews said, 'We have this hope as an anchor for the soul, firm and secure' (Heb. 6.19).

The truth we hold is bigger than our immediate experience. We must not slip out of it, but stand firm in it. We stand in the anticipation of seeing the victory Jesus has revealed in us.

The shield.

The shield was the Roman soldier's most important defence. It was made of a double thickness of wood joined together with special glue made exclusively from bull's hide. It was then covered with canvas and calfskin, and had metal strips along the edges which protected it and enabled it to be used to deflect blows from enemy swords. It had a metal boss in the centre to help deflect javelins. Every group of soldiers painted their shields different colours. In battle, the Roman soldier used it by kneeling on one knee behind it.

Our shield is 'the shield of faith with which you can extinguish all the flaming arrows of the evil one' (Eph. 6.16). Again notice it is the 'evil one' who has the offensive weapons. In the ancient world flaming arrows or fiery darts were very effective and caused many brave men to flee. If one attached itself to a soldier's shield, he was forced to lower his defence to remove it, thereby increasing his vulnerability. Anything that could catch fire was in danger. We are told by Paul that 'faith cometh by hearing, and hearing by the word of God' (Romans 10.17 KJV), and so our defence lies in believing what the word of God says about us and sheltering behind it. Satan often puts ideas into our minds that we are unloved, not accepted, disappointed, bored, lonely, bitter and many other things. If we do not have the shield of faith these things can set fire to some area of our lives and soon cause a conflagration. How many believers there are who are out of action and isolated because they received a word spoken by the enemy which set their inner fears alight. Many times I have prayed for Christian couples who have felt very cut off from other believers, who have had a sense of not fitting in and would have become more and more estranged. More often than not there was no real basis for their feelings and things changed dramatically after we had declared the truth and prayed against the deceit of the enemy. Beware Christian – the devil wants you out of action and isolated, for a lone sheep makes an easy prey. Rather, 'Resist him, standing firm in the faith' (1 Peter 5.9).

When these thoughts come we should be so certain of the truth that they are instantly extinguished.

The helmet.

'Take the helmet of salvation'. The Roman helmet was made of bronze and fitted over an iron skullcap which had a leather or cloth lining. There were often leather flaps for the ears. So effective was the helmet that very few Roman soldiers ever received head injuries; indeed a head injury was usually taken as a sign that the soldier had been cowardly and run away, throwing aside the helmet which made him so easily identifiable by the enemy.

The Christian's 'helmet' is 'salvation'. We must know that we are saved and delivered from the devil's kingdom. As the centre of our thought and reason, our heads are very vulnerable. Through our thoughts either fear and turmoil or peace and order can reign and we must therefore hold firm to the truth of our salvation.

When Satan whispers in our ears thoughts that contradict the truth of our salvation we must put the helmet firmly on. When he says, 'You're not saved, you know. You're not like the others who are real believers, you're a sham', we have to know the truth. When he claims that he has us 'firmly as ever and that things haven't changed a bit since we were saved,' we have to *know* that we have been delivered from his power into Christ's kingdom.

The sword.

'and the sword of the Spirit, which is the word of God', (v17). The Roman sword was a remarkable weapon. Previously, swords had had problems attached to them – some were too long (four to six feet was common), some too heavy, others only had a sharp point which broke off easily, and some only had one sharp edge. The Roman sword, or *machaira* was first issued to the Praetorian Guard – it had two sharp edges and a sharp point and was neither too heavy nor too long. It was an efficient and effective weapon.

The word of God is said to be 'the sword of the Spirit', and it is the weapon used by the Holy Spirit in us to fend off the many attacks made upon us. He brings the word to our attention, gives us revelations about parts of it, and brings it back to our remembrance when we need it. When Jesus was tempted in the wilderness he used verses from the book of Deuteronomy to counter the attack every time and we must be prepared to use Scripture in the same way. This means that we must be diligent in our study of God's word so that the Holy Spirit can wield it in our defence.

If we are always careful to put on the armour, we will find that when the devil or one of his soldiers comes to attack us we are well able to withstand the onslaught. Ours is the victory. Paul completes this section of Ephesians with the words, 'And pray in the spirit on all occasions with all kinds of prayers and requests. With this in mind, be alert and always keep on praying for all the saints.'

We can all pray at any time and in all circumstances and whatever type of prayer is needed, it is at our disposal.

Confession, praise, thanksgiving, intercession and petition are ours to use.

Praise be to God who has not left us defenceless on this earth, but has provided us with everything we need to 'shine like stars in the universe' (Phil. 2.15). No more should we believe Satan's lies about his power – however great it is, it is small in comparison with that revealed in Christ. The truth about us is that our life is hidden away in the one who is King of Kings and Lord of Lords, and he has given us the fulness of his victory.

9: Victory over demons

At the beginning of the second chapter I warned of the two equal and opposite errors into which believers can fall concerning demonic oppression and activity: – one is not to believe in them at all; the other is to over-emphasise them. In this chapter I want to examine the occasions when demonic influence can be identified as the root cause of our problems.

By far the majority of Christians put too little down to the activity of the unseen angelic world. The tendency is to assume that every problem has a natural cause and must be dealt with using the usual remedies. A headache is probably caused by going to bed late the previous night, or by an unusually late meal. An aspirin or Alka-Seltzer will soon bring relief. Someone who is always falling over or having accidents is just one of those people who for some reason seem to be accident-prone or who just have 'bad luck'; it's unfortunate, but that's the type of person they are. It is certainly considered a spiritual excess to bring the devil and his forces into such matters.

Yet Satan is active in these ways and wants to use them to wear down the saints. In the days in which we live his activity is very much on the increase and we need discernment if we are to live fruitful spiritual lives. Discernment is the gift given by God to detect the source of trouble in a believer's life or circumstances. If we are not able to locate the root of the problem, our remedies and solutions will be very 'hit-and-miss', and we will be like a blind boxer beating the air. Paul warns us not to put our problems automatically down to natural causes, but to consider the spiritual realm carefully.

'Our struggle is not against flesh and blood,' he says, 'but against the rulers, against the authorities, against the powers of this dark world and against the spiritual forces of evil in the heavenly realms' (Eph. 6.12). These spiritual forces, as we have seen, form the Satanic army which attempts to control the affairs of men and which would love to stop God's work. We must take account of it. We are told, 'Neither give place to the devil' (Eph. 4.27 KJV) and the fact that we have been given this command shows that it is possible for us to give place to him. The word 'place' is the Greek word *topos* and it means a region, or area of land. In English we get our word 'topology' from it. Hence we are told to make sure that no area of our lives is open to Satan's domination.

The first inkling some believers get about the possibility that the enemy might be behind some of what they are experiencing is when he overplays his hand. I noticed that whenever I had an important meeting arranged, I would wake up that morning with a splitting headache, or whenever I had to speak at a meeting I would find my throat becoming sore. Naturally I thought it was all caused by the tension I was under because of the meeting. Having accepted this for years, I then began to realise that it was happening too regularly. Even when I was looking forward to a meeting and wanted to speak, the sore throat or headache would be there. So one morning, with my head pounding, I decided to rebuke the enemy in the name of Jesus and demand that he release me. Instantly the headache went. Subsequently, I fount that this pattern was often repeated: headaches and sore throats would vanish after being rebuked, and as time went on and I continued to resist, the devil began to drop that line of attack.

A couple came to see me recently who had found that their once successful business had been in decline ever since the husband had become a Christian. Since that time every business deal had gone wrong – the turnover had declined, new ventures had flopped (at great cost), and even their attempt to buy a house had been a disaster. When they came to see me they recounted a series of failures. Yet they had prayed and committed each move to the Lord. 'Could there be a spiritual reason for what has happened?' they asked me. As far as they knew they had been in fellowship with the Lord, active in their witness and devoted in their giving, and could see no reason for their problem. As we prayed, however, we began to discern that a direct attack from the enemy had been made upon them and the Lord showed us the details. Together we stood against the enemy in the name of Jesus and asked the Lord to stop the decline and to restore what had been lost.

Just a few months later they told me that the Lord had given them new peace and prosperity and that he had provided a lump sum of money which made up for the losses they had previously incurred.

Another couple came to see me about a member of their family who was accident-prone. Everything he did seemed to lead to his being hurt or shaken in some way – buildings he was working on would collapse, car tyres would burst and they came to fear the phone ringing lest it be news of another mishap. They discerned that he was being vexed by some angelic attack and had come so that we could stand against it together. After we prayed the accidents stopped immediately, without recurrence. Examples of this type are manifold.

We must take account of the spiritual warfare in which we are involved and be ready to take action against demonic authority wherever it is revealed. In the name of the Lord Jesus Christ we have authority to stand against these things and stop them. Knowing the cause of the trouble is no use unless we also know what our own rights are in the situation.

The story is recorded in 2 Kings 6 of the king of Syria's attack upon Dothan. For some time the Syrians had wanted to defeat the king of Israel and claim some of his territory for themselves. Yet time after time whenever they planned an attack or ambush the Israelites seemed to have prior knowledge of their tactics and carefully avoided the traps that had been set. Without a success to his credit, the king of Syria had come to the conclusion that there must be a spy in his camp who was passing on information to the enemy. The enraged king summoned his officers and asked who was the spy among them but was met with the answer, 'None of us, my lord the king . . . but Elisha, the prophet who is in Israel tells the king of Israel the very words you speak in your bedroom' (v12). The Spirit of God was revealing everything to Elisha to protect the Northern Kingdom. Upon hearing this the king of Syria sent a reconnaissance party out to find where Elisha was so that he could kill him. They located him in Dothan. 'Then he sent horses and chariots and a strong force there. They went by night and surrounded the city' (v14).

It is fascinating to ponder upon the fact that as Elisha knew all that the king of Syria (=Aram) said in his 'bedroom' he would also have known of his plans to besiege and capture the city where he was staying, yet he dwelt in perfect peace and made no attempt to flee the city. It was his servant who panicked. 'Oh, my lord, what shall we do?' (v15).

Was the servant's panic due to his having too much knowledge, or too little? After all, he was the one who had seen the size of the besieging army and knew the true hopelessness of the situation. Elisha hadn't been outside his room!

The answer is, of course, that the servant's problem was *that he knew too little* and this is why Elisha prayed and said, 'O Lord, open his eyes so that he may see' (v17). When his eyes were opened he received the information he had been lacking: 'he looked and saw the hills full of horses and chariots of fire all around Elisha.' God's troops had now become visible to him. So often believers panic because, like Elisha's servant, they lack the full facts of the situation. Sometimes all we know is the problem we see, or the oppression we feel, but we don't fully appreciate God's provision for us in that situation and the result is that we panic or worry. We *must* be informed about God's provision.

Having spoken of the victory we have in Jesus and of the new place of authority we have, none of us should have problems like Elisha's servant. The devil is under our feet and legally we have the right to oppose his work. How wonderful it is that very often through demonic activity Christians are forced to wake up to the fact that they are involved in spiritual warfare and those who beforehand were ineffective suddenly become giants of faith. This is the principle of being 'more than conquerors': oppressed ignorant Christians have the scales removed from their eyes and become victorious in their risen Lord.

There is one dramatic event in the life of Jesus which demonstrates how he used demonic forces to increase the spreading of the good news. It is the account of the Gadarene swine, recorded in Mark 5. It is an incident which causes believers a great deal of trouble because they tend to concentrate on the removal of the demons into the pigs. It particularly worries those who know that it is not usually right to cast demons into animals. I cannot agree with the view of one prominent Bible teacher who says that if the demons had not been cast into the pigs but had been cast straight into Tartarus, then the man from whom they were cast out would have died. If it were true I am sure that Jesus would have raised the man from the dead. Such explanations miss the real victory and glory behind the passage. Jesus was not just content with the freeing of the demoniac from evil spirits but was so much in control of the situation that he wanted to use the demons to proclaim the Gospel. We have already established that we are more than conquerors in Jesus and this is one of the many times when Jesus demonstrated his transcendent power.

The incident occurred in the desert region of Gadara which is an area south-east of the southern tip of the Sea of Galilee. At the time of Jesus, such desert areas were the haunts of mentally ill people and demoniacs whom the residents of the towns and villages refused to have living with them. These people would scrape out a meagre existence and often resorted to robbery and attacks on wayfarers. Together with the professional bandits who also operated in regions like this they posed a major threat to travellers in the land.

Upon disembarking from the boat which had carried them across the Sea of Galilee, Jesus and the disciples were suddenly confronted by such a man rushing towards them. All attempts to chain him up had failed because of the super-strength which he possessed when the demons within him manifested themselves. Finally he had been left to rave and cut himself in an area which served as a burial place. This scarred, lacerated, bleeding man, yelling at the top of his voice in terror, ran towards the little group on the seashore. Picture the panic among the disciples as they all tried to hide behind Jesus. But Jesus didn't move. 'When he saw Jesus from a distance, he ran and fell on his knees in front of him' (v6). The important truth in this verse is that no matter how many demons a man has inside him they can never influence his free-will. The demoniac recognised immediately that this man Jesus Christ was the one who was anointed by God to set the captives free and, despite all of the evil at work within him, he rushed forward and fell on his knees. A positive response to the Lord is the first essential step before someone becomes free. It is a pointless exercise trying to help someone who doesn't really want freedom.

The demons in the man were the ones who felt fear in the presence of Jesus – not vice-versa. Not only did *he* know the fulness of the victory he was winning, but they did too. One demon spoke and said, 'What do you want with me, Jesus, Son of the Most High God? Swear to God that you won't torture me!' For Jesus was saying to him, 'Come out of this man, you evil spirit!' (v7 and 8). When Christians receive the full revelation of the victory and rights they have in Christ, it will be the evil spirits and people under their influence, eg. spiritualists, who will be bound in fear. So many believers allow themselves to be put into a place of fear and bondage by the devil when in fact he and his minions are the ones who should quake. Such dominion is part of our inheritance in Jesus.

The demon who spoke was the leader of a vast number of demons in the man and its name was 'Legion . . . for we are many' (v9). A Roman legion consisted of five to six thousand soldiers[1] and so it is clear that this was the number of demons in this one man.

When Jesus appeared in Gadara all of the demons in the man began to shake, desperate to be elsewhere. They begged Jesus not to cast them into the Abyss because they wanted to stay in the area. Demons can go from one person to another and, like the 'spirit-guides' of spiritualists who pass on from one medium to another, these demons were hoping to occupy someone else after they were thrown out of this man.

Subsequent events served as a testimony to the complete control of Jesus in this situation. Desert areas like that of Gadara had another use – not only were they dwelling-places of lunatics but they were also popular pig-rearing areas. The situation has its counterpart in Tibet before the Communist take over in 1959. Because the Tibetans believed that people could be reincarnated as animals or even insects, the killing of other creatures was completely forbidden in Lamaistic Buddhism. The Tibetans would claim that they never killed an animal for meat nor ate meat. Their problem was that in fact many of them enjoyed the occasional meat dish. To solve the dilemma most Tibetan communities would have a small number of Moslems living on the outskirts who acted as butchers and sold meat to the Tibetans under the cover of night. Although they treated the Moslems as complete outcasts, no major town was without them. To the Jews, pigs were unclean and pork was forbidden because of the Law, but some of them from time to time broke the Law and enjoyed a cut of pork. To supply the demand certain men owned herds of pigs which were kept out of sight in the desert areas. In Gadara was just such a herd.

The evil spirits, therefore, asked to be cast out into the pigs, assuming that they would then scatter into the surrounding countryside, enabling the spirits perhaps to occupy an unsuspecting passer-by. So Jesus gave them permission. Once the evil spirits had gone from the man into the animals, however, Jesus sent the pigs (which have an instinctive fear of water) plunging into the Sea of Galilee. There is no doubt that upon the death of the pigs the demons were bound in the Abyss to await their judgment.

The scene by the Sea of Galilee had now altered dramatically. Jesus and the disciples now had a man in his right mind standing among them, and just a short distance away the bodies of two thousand pigs were floating on the water. In this scene Jesus is the Mighty Conqueror, but the events which then began to occur were what turned his victory into a completely devastating disaster for the enemy.

'Those tending the pigs ran off and reported this in the town and countryside, and the people went out to see what had happened' (v14). The swine herds had to report the loss of two thousand pigs to the owner, and worse, had to tell him that they had drowned! What a stir such a thing would have caused. Jesus and the disciples just waited with the freed man and the bobbing carcasses until the crowds arrived. The demoniac would have been well-known and most of the local people would have heard of the attempts to chain him, and would have been warned of the danger he posed. 'When they came to Jesus, they saw the man who had been possessed by the legion of demons sitting there, dressed and in his right mind; and they were afraid. Those who had seen it told the people what happened to the demon-possessed man – and told about the pigs as well' (v15 and 16).

The people of this area had seen the kingly glory and power of our Saviour. He who was King of Kings and Lord of Lords had visited them and they had beheld his majesty. The incident is not just a defeat for Satan but a complete rout. We do not know how many people heard the Gospel because of this incident but the ex-demoniac returned to his undoubtedly overjoyed family and told throughout the area called Decapolis (area of ten cities) of all that Jesus had done for him.

This is the victory we have inherited and which is our birthright now that we are born again and in Christ. We are not just in a position to conquer our enemy but also to turn the tables on him and use his work for God's glory.

The early church lived in this revelation. It is interesting to find that in the book of Acts the names 'devil' and 'Satan' are each only used twice and all four references are in passages which reveal God's glory. For example, Acts 10.38: 'God anointed Jesus of Nazareth with the Holy Spirit and power, and . . . he went around doing good and healing all who were under the power of the devil.' Christians in the early church were not devil-minded, but occupied with their God and with their standing in Christ. They had become living epistles and ambassadors for

Christ who in their life together fulfilled the prophecy of Daniel 11.32, 'the people that do know their God shall be strong, and do exploits' (KJV). In our own generation Christians who know of the devil and his forces tend to put too much emphasis on him, and lack revelation of their own victory. No wonder there are so many feeble and worn-down believers today. We must reverse the tide and so live in the victory which is ours that we don't expect or invite the devil's attack. Instead, we must always be ready 'to trample on snakes and scorpions, and to overcome all the power of the enemy' (Luke 10.19). We are no longer captive to Satan's kingdom but are raised with Christ far above all principality and power (Eph. 1.20 and 21).

In the Book of Acts we see another example of our total mastery over the insidious attacks of the enemy. In Acts 16 Satan decided to make a subtle attack on Paul and his ministry. Having arrived in Philippi, the leading city in Macedonia, Paul and his companions decided to stay there several days to begin establishing the church. It was there that Satan moved: 'Once when we were going to the place of prayer, we were met by a slave girl who had a spirit by which she predicted the future. She earned a great deal of money for her owners by fortune-telling' (v16). This girl began following Paul and everywhere he went the spirit within her shouted, 'These men are servants of the Most High God, who are telling you the way to be saved' (v17). This is a very subtle attack by which the evil spirit is attempting to confuse the issue of the Gospel. To the people around who would have thought that the gospel of Jesus Christ was opposed to the devilish forms of religion already practised in Philippi, the testimony of the woman would have served to make them think that the two were compatible and, indeed, complementary. It would have maintained the woman's trade and could have led to the deception of any Christian converts.

Today if this occurred, our instant reaction would be to

cast the demons out of her, and yet interestingly, in Philippi, Paul allowed it to continue for some time. He was not impatient, but waited for the right moment. 'She kept this up for many days' (v18) and all that they preached was confirmed by the spirit of the woman. After many days Paul, Silas, Timothy and the woman would have created quite a spectacle and the crowds which gathered would have included a large number of practising spiritualists. As the crowds grew, so the confusion increased until God was ready to move. After many days Paul finally became agitated and 'he turned round and said to the spirit, "In the name of Jesus Christ I command you to come out of her!" At that moment the spirit left her' (v18). After the evil spirit had been allowed to cause confusion for such a long period of time, the final showdown would have left no doubt in the minds of the onlookers that it was opposed to the message of Jesus and that the latter was the stronger. Through the spirit's removal, its message, which was designed to confuse was exposed and with the woman totally unable to tell fortunes anymore, she became a testimony to the power of the Gospel and a reminder of the supremacy of the kingdom of light over the powers of darkness.

In this and many other passages it is clear that in no case were believers ever oppressed by demons but always demons which were oppressed by believers, and the devil could gain no advantage over our God. Even when Paul and Silas were thrown into prison, God staged his coup de théatre by arranging that the jailer himself and all his family should be saved!!

Because of the victory of Christ 'we know that in all things God works for the good of those who love him' (Romans 8.28).

We need not fear if the attacks upon us are demonically inspired because the victory of Jesus is easily sufficient to protect us and to deliver us more glorious than before.

Whether the problem is demonic infiltration into our lives, or just the influence of demonic forces around us, we have the answer – it is in Jesus Christ and all that he has provided.

We must be diligent in our prayer life to make sure that we bind the powerful forces around us. The demonic council over our lands has to be pushed back if any progress is to be made, and prayer cells devoted to the task will do more than governments or politicians for spiritual change. Only through the prevailing prayers of spiritual people can such change be accomplished.

Before God established the work to which he has committed me in Chichester, he revealed to me that the powers of evil had to be challenged and bound. I devoted myself diligently to this task when I moved down to Sussex and over a period of a year resisted the entrenched forces which would oppose the work and seek to crush it in the early stages of its growth. Over that time the spiritual climate changed and when the work began it was able to thrive rapidly.

One day while visiting Bognor Regis, which is a coastal resort six miles from Chichester, I noticed a bronze plate on the door of an office block which announced that it was the headquarters of the Rosicrucians in Great Britain. I had seen several of their advertisements in the national newspapers and knew that they were exponents of the development of man's psychic power. They claimed that many famous people like Archimedes, Leonardo da Vinci and Newton were Rosicrucians and depended on the inner power of their minds, but they never supported their claims. I knew that this was one of the centres of Satan's work in the area. So in 1972 I embarked upon a campaign of prayer to oust them. Having discharged my burden after a few months, I passed on to other things and all thoughts of Rosicrucians went from my head. It was only in 1979, while waiting in a shop, that I picked up an old

Sunday colour magazine and found an article on the Rosicrucians. To my delight I read that Bognor Regis had housed the main centre of the Rosicrucians until 1972 when they decided to move it back to the world-wide headquarters in the U.S.A. Sure enough, when I checked, the name plate was gone. Such are the victories which we will experience when we begin moving out in our authority in Christ.

In our local churches and fellowship groups we must exercise our spiritual authority because Satan is still trying to stop the work through infiltration of the church by trouble-makers. The secret always is to fight in prayer – once the victory is ours in prayer, it will not be long before it is revealed for all to see.

Wonderful joy floods the soul of one who has received the answer to his prayer as pressure and anxiety lift and heavenly truth dawns in each area of his life. If only we will dare to challenge the devil and his evil armies and stand on the truth that they are already disarmed, we will see them retreat before us.

10: Pulling down the strongholds

The Bible testifies about king Josiah that 'he did what was right in the eyes of the Lord and walked in the ways of his father David, not turning aside to the right or to the left' (2 Chron. 34.2). For fifty-seven years, during the reign of king Manasseh and his son Amon, the kingdom of Judah had been in spiritual decline. Within a few years of his accession to the throne Manasseh had undone all the good things done by Hezekiah, his father. He re-established the centres of idolatry; allowed Baal to be worshipped in the house of the Lord; practised human sacrifice; consulted mediums and soothsayers and even called his son after the Egyptian god Amon. Together, Manasseh and his son were two of the worst and most cruel kings ever to reign.

Faced with such appalling spiritual conditions, Josiah determined in his heart that the decline would cease, and that God's ways would be re-established. When he was only twelve he began destroying the idols and altars in the land and at the age of eighteen he began repairing the temple of the Lord. As the work on the temple advanced, Hilkiah the priest found a discarded scroll of the word of God. It had been neglected for so long that the knowledge of God's feasts had ceased in the land, and God who watches over his word to perform it (Jer. 1.12) only brought the scroll to light when godly men began to rule again. Once it was read to the king, he began to re-introduce its ordinances and restore God's perfect ways in the land.

Today God is seeking such a restoration in us as individuals and in his Church, and again it will be through a revelation of the word of God that such a restoration will come. When Paul commands 'let the word of Christ dwell in you richly' (Col. 3.16) he is exhorting us to be occupied fully with all the truth concerning Jesus Christ and his work. The things that are true, now that Jesus Christ is risen and ascended, are the things that must occupy our thoughts and govern our lives. It is no use our being blown about by 'every wind of doctrine' (Eph 4.14 KJV); we must know the truth and allow it to stabilise us.

A believer's mind is a battlefield over which the enemy strives for control. It will either enable him to be strong in his faith or will be his enemy. Paul told the Ephesians to 'walk not as other Gentiles walk, in the vanity of their mind, having the understanding darkened, being alienated from the life of God through the ignorance that is in them' (Eph. 4.17 and 18 KJV). Non-Christians have no enlightenment in the things of God because they are not born again and therefore do not have the Holy Spirit in them. It is disgraceful if regenerate believers walk around in the same blindness as them. Unfortunately, all too many believers do – their minds are filled with nonsense or lies which contradict the principles of truth revealed in God's word and so they find themselves in bondage.

The word 'vanity' means 'emptiness, fruitlessness, futility or purposelessness' and all of these words describe the non-Christian philosophy and manner of life. As we have seen in previous chapters fallen man can achieve nothing but short-term satisfaction; in the end any imagined purpose vanishes like a mist leaving him frustrated and unfulfilled. Such is not the lot of a believer. Everything we do in God's work has eternal consequences – the times spent in prayer have everlasting results; the lives we lay down for him are restored one hundredfold in heaven and are used for the extension of his kingdom on earth; even the money we give is 'invested' in that God gives vast interest on it – 'good measure, pressed down, shaken together and running over' (Luke 6.38). Through Jesus Christ the futility of the fall is overcome, and all we do through faith in him in our daily lives takes on eternal significance. As Jim Elliot, the missionary murdered by the Auca Indians, said before his death, 'He is no fool who gives what he cannot keep to gain that which he cannot lose.'

If, like non-Christians, we are vain in our thinking then we are liable to fall prey to the world's propaganda and to be taken in by its false promises of happiness. Many, many believers waste their lives striving in the world for the fulfilment and happiness that only God can give. Their problem began in their thinking.

The word 'vanity' always reminds me of a vacuum. By reducing pressure in one area, things around press in upon it and attempt to fill the emptiness. If a believer has a vacuum in his thinking then like a vacuum-cleaner he will pick up all kinds of rubbish. All the ideas and lies of the world will press in upon him and soon occupy his thinking. All of us need to have our minds occupied with something and it will either be the standards and truths of God, or the philosophy of the world. Proverbs 23.7 tells us of man that 'as he thinketh in his heart, so is he' (KJV), and what occupies our thinking will determine our behaviour. Isaiah 55.8 '"my thoughts are not your thoughts, neither are your ways my ways" declares the Lord', and if we are to be occupied with the truth we have to be occupied with the word of God and with walking in all it says. It was not many months after I was converted that I found that God and I had fundamental differences in our opinions and as he declares that 'I the Lord do not change' (Mal. 3.6) it became clear to me that I would have to change. In many areas it took me months to be willing to be convinced by the Holy Spirit and even now as I go on with God I find more and more of my ideas having to bow the knee to him. It is in vogue today to sit in judgment on the word of God and to accept it or reject it according to whether or not it suits our logic. During the period that I was a teacher, I heard many people speaking in the school assembly. Very often I found them basing their talks on certain passages of Scripture but rejecting any verse in them with which they disagreed. It occurs most frequently in Matthew 25.31–46 where the social gospellers concentrate on the need to give the hungry food, and the thirsty drink, but then reject v41 and v46 where those who fail to do these things are said to be 'cursed' and thrown into 'eternal fire'. They don't believe in eternal judgment and so they choose to disregard these verses.

In fact it is not we who should sit in judgment on the word of God, but the word of God which should judge our beliefs. 'The word of God is living and active, sharper than any double-edged sword . . . *it judges* the thoughts and attitudes of the heart' (Heb. 4.12). Our thinking must be brought into line with what it declares and we must not try to change it to suit ourselves. He knows more than us and we must recognise that 'the fear of the Lord is the beginning of wisdom' (Prov. 9.10).

We must think the thoughts of God about ourselves and our lives if we are to see his victory in our lives and rise above the experiences of the world. We are commanded 'Do not conform any longer to the pattern of this world, but be transformed' (Romans 12.2), and the passage then goes on to tell us how to be transformed . . . 'by the renewing of your mind'. It is the only way in which we can shine happily and brightly for God in a world which surrounds us with its pessimism, negativism and futility. The world is bowed down with fear, uncertainty and doubt but our hope is in God and our thinking must be occupied with heavenly reality – even the 'mind of Christ' (1 Cor. 2.16 KJV).

The Holy Spirit is in us to reveal the truth to us as Jesus promised: 'But when he, the Spirit of truth, comes, he will guide you into all truth' (John 16.13) and his promise is that 'then you will know the truth, and the truth will set you free' (John 8.32).

'We have *not* received the spirit of the world but the Spirit who is from God, that we may understand what God has freely given us' (1 Cor. 2.12).

Our problem derives from the time before we were born again. A Christian who is saved at the age of twenty-five has already had twenty-five years of worldly training. If his parents have been non-Christians they will have taught him how the world acts and reacts, and in his formative years he will have picked up their behaviour and attitudes. His education and his own experience will have compounded the effect. Indeed, every morning his fallen nature, aided to a greater or lesser extent by the devil, has been dictating to him how he should think and feel for the day. Upon becoming a Christian these old habits die hard, but immediately the Spirit of God begins to work so that the new creation which is of Christ begins to have an effect. If the Christian is a willing partner, receiving encouragement and example from his fellow believers, then, before many years the transformation will have spread to every area, so that not only is he a new creation inside, but every facet of his life shows it. Sometimes areas will be changed sovereignly by the Spirit of God; sometimes we have to 'put off your old self' and actively 'put on the new' (Eph. 4.22 and 24); and sometimes our lives are transformed as we receive new revelation from the word. Most Christians find that they experience a combination of these.

Wherever we see an attitude or idea which contradicts the word, it is part of our responsibility to deal with it.

Paul portrays this graphically: 'For though we live in the world, we do not wage war as the world does. The weapons we fight are not the weapons of the world. On the contrary, they have divine power to demolish strongholds.

We demolish arguments and every pretension that sets itself up against the knowledge of God, and *we take captive* every thought to make it obedient to Christ' (2 Cor. 10.3–5).

Paul frequently uses incidents in history to demonstrate spiritual truth and here he bases his ideas on events which were well-known at the time he wrote, but which few of us know about today. They concerned the food supplies of the Roman Empire. About one hundred years before Paul wrote these words the Mediterranean had been swarming with pirates who disrupted trade and sometimes succeeded in severing communications with the Roman outposts. Rome depended upon the countries at the eastern end of the Mediterranean for its supplies of grain and in 67 BC., the greatest problem Rome faced was the high price of corn, caused by the shortage which continual piracy had created. Once their pockets had been touched the voters of Rome clamoured for the neutralisation of the pirates.

These pirates, who numbered thousands, lived in fortresses or strongholds which lined the cliffs of Cilicia (the southern coast of Turkey) and they retreated to these after their skirmishes. The Roman general, Pompey, was given the task of breaking the pirates' stranglehold and 'a powerful force equipped with siege-engines and prepared for all kinds of mountain warfare was made ready.'[1] His forces sailed to the Cilician coasts and by means of the siege-engines they dismantled the fortresses and pushed them over the cliffs into the sea. One hundred and twenty of these eyrie-like strongholds were destroyed and ten thousand pirates taken captive and paraded through Rome.

Just as the Roman citizens were denied food, oil, wine and the other goods which made life in Rome legendary for its luxuriance, so we believers are rendered poor by wrong thinking and false ideas which rob us of the glorious provision which the work of Jesus has made available to us. These things must be tackled though it often takes time because they have become entrenched in our minds over a period of years. Chance remarks made by parents or by teachers and fellow pupils at school can often determine how we view ourselves and we need to allow what the Bible says of us to sink deeply into our thinking, so that we begin to see ourselves as we truly are in Jesus.

The more I have talked in depth with people, the more surprised I have been by the wrong ideas we often have of ourselves. Even outwardly confident people are often covering up deep-seated feelings of inferiority or inadequacy. If these strongholds are not removed and the thoughts 'taken captive' then they will sap our true Christian confidence.

Most of us as Christians have high moral values and when we fail to reach them it is very difficult to believe that we are forgiven and therefore to forgive ourselves. It was very common for me as a young Christian to confess the same sin for several days on end. I could never forgive myself for it and so couldn't really believe that God had forgiven me. Sometimes I used to think it would be easier if God really punished me – at least then I could feel as if it was dealt with. How hard it is for the natural man to receive forgiveness by grace. Nor are we helped by our failure to realise that Jesus was punished in full in our stead for each and every sin. I remember well the day when, after confessing one particular sin for about eight days, the Lord spoke to me and said, 'What sin?' and I began to realise that my unbelief was preventing me from receiving forgiveness in my experience.

'As far as the east is from the west, so far has he removed our transgressions from us' (Psalm 103.12).

'I, even I, am he who blots out your transgressions, for my own sake, and remembers your sins no more' (Isaiah 43.25).

They were gone but I hadn't received it because my own moral sense hadn't felt cleansed.

A few months after this God gave me a graphic example of what blotting out our sins really meant. As a geography teacher it was part of my job to teach my fifteen-year-old 'O' level group about the countries of north-west Europe. Having completed a detailed study of France I was ready to progress to Belgium, but decided to have an oral test to make sure the basic geographical facts had been assimilated. So I spent a large part of one lunch hour drawing a beautiful map on the blackboard. Every colour of chalk was used – the mountains, the rivers, the main cities, the major ports, the nuclear power stations, the oil pipelines and anything else I could clearly mark was put in. When I left to go to the staffroom, a masterpiece of which Mercator himself would have been proud, adorned the board.

By the time I arrived for my first class of the afternoon, however, it had vanished. One of the more helpful fifteen-year-olds, knowing that we were due to begin studying Belgium had decided to save me work by cleaning all the boards. So careful was he that he even went over his work with a damp cloth to make sure that a really new start could be made that afternoon. Imagine my horror when I arrived back in the classroom; yet I couldn't do anything but thank the boy for trying to be helpful. The map was gone beyond recall. How stupid it would have been if I had carried on as if it were still there, demanding answers from the class with reference to a completely blank blackboard. Yet as the Lord showed me, I was doing just that with him – carrying on as if his removal of my sin was not as effective as the work of a fifteen-year-old with a blackboard rubber. We must learn that having confessed a sin we can and indeed must move on. If we dwell upon a sin for too long we are simply giving it more ground in our life and we'll become pre-occupied with it, obsessed by it and eventually so negative that we will be unable to bear the weight of it. Having confessed it we must acknowledge that 'he is faithful and just and will forgive us our sins and purify us from all unrighteousness' (1 John 1.9). Then we must get so pre-occupied with Jesus himself that we become determined to devote ourselves to him with renewed vigour. 'But one thing I do: Forgetting what is behind and straining towards what is ahead, I press on . . .' (Phil. 3.13). This is the walk of faith.

This also covers our former lives. There is no need to be haunted by a past that is erased; when we were born again we not only became new creatures but the truth is that 'the old has gone, the new has come!' (2 Cor. 5.17). We can therefore walk away as free men and women. We can claim complete freedom and deliverance from whatever has happened to us in the past. God rebuked the Jews in Ezekiel's day for their constant use of the proverb 'The fathers eat sour grapes, and the children's teeth are set on edge' (Ezek. 18.2). God told them, 'As surely as I live, declares the Sovereign Lord, you will no longer quote this proverb in Israel' (v3). If he could say it to them, how much more should he say it to us who are in Christ and who therefore share his past.

All of these problems come from our wrong thinking and unbelief. His forgiveness is so wide and his power so great that we can leave our sin completely with him. 'Therefore, there is now no condemnation for those who are in Christ Jesus' (Rom. 8.1).

Needless to say, Satan will take any opportunity we give him in this area and make capital out of it. As we have seen he is the 'accuser of the brethren' and so we must know the answer to his accusation.

In Zechariah 3 we have the description of a scene which occurs every day in heaven. Having failed to stop the rebuilding of the temple in 518 B.C., Satan changed his tactics and began to accuse the newly appointed high priest, Joshua, whose job it was to serve in the temple. 'Then he showed me Joshua the high priest standing before the angel of the Lord (Jehovah)' (v1). He was undoubtedly serving God in his priestly capacity when Satan appeared to do his evil work of accusation. In a play on words Zechariah stated literally that Satan was there to Satanise him. 'The angel of the Lord' is one of the titles used of the Lord Jesus when he appeared in the Old Testament and here, in one of the many passages which reveal the Trinity, the angel of Jehovah is said to be Jehovah himself. 'The Lord said to Satan, "The Lord rebuke you, Satan! The Lord, who has chosen Jerusalem, rebuke you! Is not this man a burning stick snatched from the fire?"' (v2).

Joshua was being attacked, the angel of the Lord is his defence, and Satan was his accuser. Before a word can be said by Satan he was rebuked by the Lord who then gave certain commands to those standing around. 'Now Joshua was dressed in filthy clothes as he stood before the angel. The angel said to those who were standing before him, "Take off his filthy clothes." Then he said to Joshua, "See, I have taken away your sin, and I will put rich garments on you"' (v3 and 4).

We have become partakers of the same grace. We, like Joshua, are guilty sinners: Satan accuses us, and Jesus acts in our defence. 'If anybody does sin, we have one who speaks to the Father in our defence – Jesus Christ, the Righteous One' (1 John 2.1). Again, the first thing that happens is that Satan is rebuked and excluded. Because we, who are born again, are God's children, our misdemeanours are a family affair. Satan is not part of that family and is therefore immediately cast out. No one allows neighbours to join in family disputes. Furthermore, Jesus presents to the Father his own work for us in taking our filthy garments on himself on the Cross, and giving to us his garment of righteousness (see 2 Cor. 5.21).

We stand, therefore, at peace with God, without his condemnation.

The trouble is that, having been kicked out of court, Satan often sends one of his angels to whisper one of his lies in our ear. 'God's had enough'. 'That was the last straw'. 'You're too bad to be a Christian'.

These thoughts must be demolished with our confession of the truth. Then we are free.

With the truth occupying our minds we will know exactly how we stand with God at any moment. We belong to God and have been bought with the price of his blood (1 Cor. 6.19 and 20). We have been 'qualified . . . to share in the inheritance of the saints in the kingdom of light. For he has rescued us from the dominion of darkness and brought us into the kingdom of the Son he loves' (Col. 1.12 and 13). Satan may lie and say we are still under his control, but that this is not so is clearly shown in Job 1. Here Satan appears before God and when asked by God where he has come from, he answers boastfully, 'From roaming through the earth and going to and fro in it' (Job 1.7). He uses an idiom which meant that the earth and its fulness belonged to him – it would be used for example of a nobleman viewing his estate. It is a boast which is not true. God disarms him with one question. 'Have you considered my servant Job?' (v8). This was designed to remind Satan that Job was a believer and therefore belonged to God. We must remind Satan that we too belong to God and we must take captive any thought to the contrary in our own minds.

The truth about us is that we are now free men whose home and allegiance is in heaven. If we set our minds on the earth, or on the things of the earth, we will experience the deathly principle which is so much a part of this world. The truth is that nothing can now enslave us unless we either remain in ignorance of our freedom or choose to be enslaved. Through Jesus Christ the truth concerning us is that the world about us has no mastery over us; we are no longer forced to commit sin because of our fallen state and the angelic world need not dominate us any longer for it is under our feet. The word of God which reveals these truths must be our confession.

'May I never boast except in the cross of our Lord Jesus Christ, through which the world has been crucified to me, and I to the world' (Gal. 6.14).

'You died . . . to the basic principles of this world' (Col. 2.20).

You have 'an inheritance that can never perish, spoil or fade – kept in heaven for you' (1 Peter 1.4).

'Those who belong to Christ Jesus have crucified the sinful nature with its passions and desires' (Gal. 5.24).

'For we know that our old self was crucified with him so that the body of sin might be rendered powerless, that we should no longer be slaves to sin' (Rom. 6.6).

'Count yourselves dead to sin but alive to God in Christ Jesus. Therefore do not let sin reign in your mortal body so that you obey its evil desires' (Rom. 6.11 and 12).

'Resist the devil, and he will flee from you' (James 4.7). We are free to choose and we must use our will for God's purpose and side with him.

'It is for freedom that Christ has set us free. Stand firm, then, and do not let yourselves be burdened again by a yoke of slavery' (Gal. 5.1).

On the positive side we must train our minds to expect what is rightfully ours. Because Jesus has reversed the effects of the fall of Adam, we can expect to receive many of the blessings that were originally his, and more. Adam had the right of dominion and as believers we should expect a greater degree of authority in our circumstances than we had before we were saved. Jesus, the last Adam, exercised total dominion in the created realm and we should expect to see something of that manifested in our lives. Jesus healed the sick but there is no reference to his experiencing sickness himself. Paul tells us that 'if the

Spirit of him who raised Jesus from the dead is living in you, he who raised Christ from the dead will also give life to your mortal bodies through his Spirit, who lives in you' (Rom. 8.11).

We can expect a toning up of our physical condition and an increase in our enjoyment and appreciation of all God's blessings, 'who richly provides us with everything for our enjoyment' (1 Tim. 6.17). My own father became interested in the Gospel because the thin-faced, pale, serious son he saw off to University, came home a few months later smiling, relaxed and with a healthy colour.

We should move out more in faith to control our surroundings. Our faith should be applied in every direction from praying for our children in the womb, to praying for bumper harvests in our gardens; from claiming good health, to commanding peace into our homes. God delights in those who dare to move in faith and simplicity, and how Satan would love to get us entangled in confusion. The Bible warns about this: 'But I fear, lest by any means, as the serpent beguiled Eve through his subtilty, so your minds should be corrupted from the simplicity that is in Christ' (2 Cor. 11.3 KJV).

I have learned to be more simple. When I heard of an American minister who believed that the Lord would adjust the weather wherever he went so that he could be 'at home' everywhere, my scepticism was unbounded. When he arrived in England for a fortnight's trip, therefore, I decided to check the weather statistics against those of his home town. The sun began to shine and the temperature rose from the morning his plane touched down at Heathrow, and it didn't rain again until the day he left! It was a bitter pill for me to swallow – to have to admit that instead of my meteorological training being able to debunk the man's claims, it had served only to support them. Actually it was my unbelief and wrong notion of who our God is which was being challenged and changed. Up to that time my God had been God of the spiritual realm only, rather than a God who interested himself with the minutia of our physical existence. Like the Arameans of old, I had to learn that our God was God of the hills and of the valleys (see 1 Kings 20.23–28). I began to pray about these things and started to move out in faith.

When I read that the children of Israel in the wilderness were blessed with clothes and shoes that didn't wear out, I began to claim a reduced rate of wear and tear for the things I owned and the results on clothes, tyres and mechanical things have been remarkable. Being simple in our relationship with him is the key which will open many doors in our lives. The world, the flesh and the devil oppose us and our faith may have to be sown for some time before we see any results, but we are not those who shrink back (Heb. 10.38). The Holy Spirit tells us, as Christians to, 'Be fruitful and increase in number; fill the earth and subdue it' (Gen. 1.28).

More than this, however, Jesus has opened up to us all the blessings which God promised to those who love him and keep his commandments. Jesus fulfilled every part of the law of God, and in him we receive the benefits of his life. This is outlined in Romans 8.3 and 4, 'And so he condemned sin and sinful man, *in order that the righteous requirements of the law might be fully met in us*, who do not live according to the sinful nature but according to the Spirit.' Because we live in him, and he in us, the law has been fulfilled in us. This means that the blessings are available to us.

Deuteronomy 28.1–14 outlines the blessings and it enables us to detail what we can legitimately expect.

Geographical Blessings
Blessed in the city
Blessed in the country
Blessed when you come in

Blessed when you go out
Blessed in the land he gives us

National Blessings
Nation set on high and known as a godly people
Admired and feared by other nations
Enemies will be defeated
Climate will be good – so no disastrous harvests
We will lend to other nations, but borrow from none
We will be the head but not the tail; top and never the bottom.

Abundant Prosperity
Children will be blessed
Crops will be blessed
Animals will be blessed
Buying and baking will be blessed
Storehouses will be blessed
Work of our hands will be blessed

We must expect these not on the basis of our good deeds, but on the sure foundation of Christ's completed work.

Because such pre-occupation with Christ and all his work is alien to the natural man, the Holy Spirit trains us step by step in the way. We must see all that happens to us as part of that training process which will ultimately equip us for the glorious task God has for us in the age to come. There are no accidents with our God and so we must not panic in adversity but keep our minds fully on him. 'Consider it pure joy, my brothers, whenever you face trials of many kinds, because you know that the testing of your faith develops perseverance. Perseverance must finish its work so that you may be mature and complete, not lacking anything' (James 1.2–4).

Paul had learned to be content in all circumstances and

in Philippians 1.12 he expresses the mind of Christ about his imprisonment. 'Now I want you to know, brothers, that what has happened to me has really served to advance the Gospel'. He is not bemoaning his lot or whimpering bitterly. 'Why me, Lord?' – he has his mind on God's glory and knows that because God is Lord of all, this will work for his good and for the good of the Gospel. The word 'to advance' here, or as the King James has it 'furtherance', is the Greek word *prokope* and it is the word for a woodcutter. Often an advance party of woodcutters would be sent ahead of a Roman army to clear the path before them and remove any fallen trees so that their progress was unhindered. Paul, imprisoned in Rome and chained day and night to a soldier, announced his predicament would make the progress of the Gospel more rapid. Paul was right. Not only did the church in Rome become more bold and thrive because of his presence; not only did the publicity of it bring Christianity to the notice of the Romans, but many of the best Roman troops, the Praetorian guard, and even members of Caesar's household, were converted. Indeed, Paul ends his letter to the Philippians with the words, 'All the saints send you greetings, especially those who belong to Caesar's household' (Phil. 4.22).

Someone who has been trained by God is immovable. John, who was leading a revival in Ephesus, didn't wail and kick against God when he was arrested, but went to Patmos rejoicing in the Lord. There he was the only member of the congregation when Jesus preached his last message. John wrote it down and today it is called the book of Revelation.

God's promise is that 'Thou wilt keep him in perfect peace, whose mind is stayed on thee: because he trusteth in thee.' It is followed by a command, 'Trust ye in the Lord forever: for in the Lord JEHOVAH is everlasting strength' (Isaiah 26.3 and 4 KJV).

Perhaps it is David who best illustrates God's plan for us. When he faced Goliath he did so with training in God behind him. He had seen his God's power many times in the daily routine of his life, and because of those incidents, his faith had developed. His confidence was not in himself but in God, and he was pre-occupied with God's glory. His indignation – 'Who is this uncircumcised Philistine that he should defy the armies of the living God?' (1 Sam. 17.26) – was not as his brother Eliab thought, the conceited boastings of a teenager, but the expression of amazement from one who knew his God. When Saul points out to him that he cannot fight Goliath because he is an untrained boy, David's reply is profound: 'But David said to Saul, "Your servant has been keeping his father's sheep. When a lion or a bear came and carried off a sheep from the flock, I went after it, struck it and rescued the sheep from its mouth. When it turned on me, I seized it by its hair, struck it and killed it. Your servant has killed both the lion and the bear; this uncircumcised Philistine will be like one of them, because he has defied the armies of the living God. The LORD who delivered me from the paw of the lion and the paw of the bear will deliver me from the hand of this Philistine"' (v34–37).

Finally, as he met Goliath, he said that he came against him 'in the name of the Lord Almighty, the God of the armies of Israel, whom you have defied' (v45), and his confession was that 'All those gathered here will know that it is not by sword or spear that the LORD saves; for the battle is the LORD'S' (v47). David was tearing down the stronghold which opposed God and which had produced fear and defeat in the soldiers of Israel. We need to do the same, to 'gird up the loins of your mind' (1 Peter 1.13 KJV). This analogy brings to our minds the people of the ancient world who wore long flowing robes. Around their waists they would wear a big belt called a girdle. When they had to move swiftly, or complete an energetic task, they would pull up the robes and tuck them into the girdle so that their legs were free. A toga looks very attractive but it is an emcumbrance when running a marathon. So the thoughts of our minds have to be under control and not in the way to trip us up. By filling our minds with truth, and casting forth false ideas we are fulfilling God's command: 'Prepare your minds for action' (1 Peter 1.13).

The fact is that we stand complete in Jesus and not in our own strength; we have his victory and have put on Christ; He is the Mighty Conqueror and we are his people. The battle is the Lord's and he has won it. 'Blessed is the man who trusts in the LORD, whose confidence is in him' (Jer. 17.7). We may rest in his love and provision. What a rich and inexhaustible store of blessing and gladness he has in reserve for the heart that thus rests in him.

11: Operation footstool

God's plan of redemption was designed to redeem man from the guilt and power of sin and to restore him, not just to the former position which Adam had in Eden, but to one far higher. Although Adam was created lord of the earth he was made lower than the angelic realm, but we in Christ, while maintaining lordship over the earth, have also been raised above the angelic orders.

'In bringing many sons to glory it was fitting that God . . . should make the Pioneer of their salvation perfect through suffering. Both the one who makes men holy and those who are made holy are of the same family. So Jesus is not ashamed to call them brothers' (Heb. 2.10 and 11).

Having seen his victory over sin, death, hell and the devil we are now presented with a dilemma. When we 'set our hearts on the things above, where Christ is seated at the right hand of God' (Col. 3.1) his complete dominion is clear to see. But when we look around us in the world we still see the fall on every hand and Satan's angelic council deceiving the nations. In the word of God we see the same apparent contradiction. On the one hand it is said that 'the earth is the Lord's and the fulness thereof' (Psalm 24.1 KJV) and that 'He rules for ever by his power' (Psalm 66.7), while on the other hand Satan is called 'prince of this world' (John 14.30) and 'the god of this world' (2 Cor. 4.4 KJV).

How do we resolve it? The answer is that, although Satan's rule is apparent, it is still under God's overall authority and he it is who has the final say. He has set a time, for example, when he will again directly intervene into the affairs of man and bring to an end Satan's temporary period of dominance. Satan is completely powerless to stop it, or even to delay it by one hour.

Even now while Satan seems to be enjoying some success in the earth, God has set limits over which Satan may not pass. He may claim omnipotence and frighten some believers into ascribing too much power to him, but in fact the scope of his power is circumscribed and its duration limited. The time left to him is very short.

From the book of Job we can see how God actually uses Satan. In it, Satan's claim that he would have total allegiance from humanity if only God would allow him to apply enough pressure to them, is exposed as bogus. At the beginning of the account Satan taunts God by saying that if ever his blessings were removed, Job's devotion to him would vanish like a mist. 'Very well, then,' God says to Satan, 'everything he has is in your hands, but on the man himself do not lay a finger' (Job 1.12). When that fails Satan has to apply to God for permission to do more. 'Very well, then,' says God again, 'he is in your hands; but you must spare his life' (Job 2.6). Satan failed miserably in his experiment and in so doing left us with the certain knowledge that our God reigns. The resulting jewel of revelation that we call the book of Job provides us with a clear exposition of Satan's subservience to God.

Satan's attacks are also used by God to strengthen believers. When Jesus warned Peter that Satan had desired to sift him like wheat he did not say that he had prevented Satan, but that he had prayed that Peter's faith would not fail. Then he proclaimed that, afterwards, Peter would be of greater service than ever and that he would strengthen his brethren (Luke 22.31–32).

On a more sombre note, God uses Satan to discipline both believers and unbelievers. The church at Corinth was told by Paul to deal with an unrepentant immoral man by handing him over to Satan, 'so that the sinful nature may be destroyed and his spirit saved on the day of the Lord' (1 Cor. 5.5). It is wonderful to see the outcome in 2 Corinthians 2.6 and 7. Here, the same man is back in fellowship and Paul is exhorting them that he should be forgiven. Satan was just an instrument God used to perform the work.

A more unfortunate example is described in 1 Kings 22 where Jehoshaphat, king of Judah, made an unholy alliance with the evil king Ahab of Israel to wrest land from the king of Aram. God had chosen this time to judge Ahab and take his life and so when Ahab collected the prophets together to ask whether his plans would be blessed God ensured that their answer was 'Go . . . for the Lord will give it into the king's hand' (v6). The religious hypocrisy of Ahab who had killed many of the Lord's prophets and opposed his ways was a major sin. Before taking the advice, Jehoshaphat asked if there was another prophet who could be brought before them. There remained only Micaiah whom Ahab hated because he would not become a puppet but was steadfastly faithful to the word of God. Micaiah arrived, and, knowing that Ahab wanted his own way, sarcastically said, 'Attack and be victorious . . . for the Lord will give it into the king's hand' (v15). Ahab picked up the sarcasm and demanded that the prophet said what he really thought. Ahab didn't accept it but interpreted it as a personal insult. But Micaiah continued, 'I saw the Lord sitting on his throne with all the host of heaven standing round him on his right and on his left. And the Lord said, "Who will lure Ahab into attacking Ramoth Gilead and going to his death there?" One suggested this, and another that. Finally, a spirit came forward, stood before the Lord and said, "I will lure him".

"By what means?" the Lord asked.

"I will go out and be a lying spirit in the mouths of all his prophets," he said.

"You will succeed in luring him," said the Lord. "Go and do it."

So now the Lord has put a lying spirit in the mouths of all these prophets of yours. The Lord has decreed disaster for you' (1 Kings 22.19–23).

The point is that God, who is sovereign, is in perfect control of the universe and therefore, no matter how much Satan opposes his plan, God's will is always done.

Today God permits the angelic opposition to his plan to run its course, but its end is near. In 1 Timothy 6.15 and 16 there is a wonderful description of God which confirms his incomparable greatness and supremacy: 'who is the blessed and only Potentate, the King of Kings, and Lord of Lords; who only hath immortality, dwelling in the light which no man can approach unto; whom no man hath seen, nor can see: to whom be honour and power everlasting. Amen' (KJV).

The title 'only Potentate' expresses the truth which all believers need to keep in mind. The word Potentate means someone with ruling power and Paul firmly states that God is the only one with this power. In human history there have been many great men and tyrants who have exerted power over millions and instilled fear into countless hearts. Alexander the Great, the Roman Emperors, Ghengis Kan, Mussolini and Hitler are numbered among them. But their power has been limited both in time and extent. It is sobering to realise that Hitler, who became Chancellor of Germany in 1933, had committed suicide only twelve years later in 1945. His power was so limited that he couldn't even guarantee good weather for his holidays or prevent a common cold affecting him. Alexander the Great conquered kingdoms and yet he is believed to have died of malaria as a result of a mosquito bite. He reigned for only eleven years.

Our God's reign lasts forever and there is nothing that is beyond his control. He reigns now, even though for a short season he permits Satan and his forces to hold sway, and his plan is that all power and authority will be in the hands of Jesus. 'And he (God) made known to us the mystery of his will according to his good pleasure, which he purposed in Christ, to be put into effect when the times will have reached their fulfilment – to bring all things in heaven and on earth together under one head, even Christ' (Eph. 1.9 and 10). When several countries form an alliance with one another they often 'put all things under one head' by appointing one man to be in charge of the combined forces. Under him all the other generals and admirals put their authority. At present, the earth is administered by those upstart angels whom Satan appointed to their position, but the day is not far hence when they will be overthrown and all authority put under the sole control of Jesus.

God ordained that a man should rule his creation and his words to Adam that he should 'subdue' the earth, and 'rule over' the animals were an expression of his perfect plan. Satan's present rulership is contrary to God's eternal purpose. 'To which of the angels did God ever say, "Sit at my right hand until I make your enemies a footstool for your feet?"' (Heb. 1.13). He didn't say it to any angel and certainly not to the cherub Satan. 'It is *not* to angels that he has subjected the world to come, about which we are speaking. But there is a place where someone has testified: '"What is man that you are mindful of him, the Son of man that you care for him? You made him a little lower than the angels; you crowned him with glory and honour and put everything under his feet"' (Heb. 2.5–8).

Satan hates the reminder of these words from the Psalms for they show clearly how he has usurped the throne God gave to man. We are within our legal rights to say to Satan, 'On whose authority do you try to control my life and circumstances?'

The man Jesus Christ has attained to all that God

planned for man and it is he who stands as our guarantee that God's purpose for Adam will be carried out, even though we don't see it yet.

The writer to the Hebrews continues: 'In putting everything under him (man), God left nothing that is not subject to him. Yet at present we do not see everything subject to him. *But we see Jesus*, who was made a little lower than the angels, now crowned with glory and honour' (Heb. 2.8 and 9). Being occupied with Christ is the key, for in him we see the fulfilment of God's promises to us – he overcame death and rose to show us that we need not fear. He is seated on the right hand of God the Father to show that the gulf between God and man has been bridged and that we, too can approach the throne of God. And God's promise that the whole earth will be the footstool of Jesus shows that God's purposes for man are 'Yea and Amen'. In him we see it all complete. 'Therefore, holy brothers, who share in the heavenly calling, fix your thoughts on Jesus' (Heb. 3.1).

All thrones in the ancient world had footstools. King Solomon's throne is described in 2 Chronicles 9.17–19: 'Then the king made a great throne inlaid with ivory and overlaid with pure gold. The throne had six steps, and a footstool of gold was attached to it. On both sides of the seat were armrests, with a lion standing beside each of them. Twelve lions stood on the six steps, one at either end of each step.' The footstool was not really for the king to rest his feet, but rather for those who came into his presence to put their heads on as they bowed down. The sign of complete subjection was the foot of the victor on the neck of the vanquished, and by putting one's head on the footstool one professed to be the king's slave. The loyal subjects and allies did it voluntarily, but the captured enemies had to be forced to so kneel. In Philippians 2.9–11 we have this image used. 'Therefore God exalted him to the highest place and gave him the name that is above every name, that at the name of Jesus every knee should bow, in heaven and on earth and under the earth, and every tongue confess that Jesus Christ is Lord, to the glory of God the Father.' The same thought is expressed in Romans 14.11 and Isaiah 45.23.

Nothing in the created realm will be exempt. All creatures in the universe fall into one of these three categories: those in heaven, those in earth and those under the earth. This includes all people, whether believers or unbelievers; all angels, whether holy or fallen, and every other creature. Some will gladly bow the knee and confess him as Lord, but the unbelievers and fallen angels, including Satan will do so under subjugation. The word 'confess' means 'to speak the same thing', 'to admit' or 'to agree', and so the passage confirms that the day is coming when even those who have refused his salvation will have to agree that Jesus Christ is Lord. What a fearful day for them. How it should increase our prayer life and urgency to witness when we consider that the headmasters, bank managers, lawyers, bosses and relatives with whom we come into contact will one day be bowing the knee. Tyrants like Emperor Nero, Stalin and Hitler; great leaders like Churchill and John F. Kennedy; kings and queens, and even atheist philosophers, such as Bertrand Russell, will on that day bow the knee. No wonder God replies to the self important struttings of the godless with the words: ' "Why do the nations rage and the peoples plot in vain?" The One enthroned in heaven laughs; the Lord scoffs at them. Then he rebukes them in his anger and terrifies them in his wrath, saying, "I have installed my King on Zion, my holy hill"' (Psalm 2.1 and 4–6). At the moment, Christ's domination has not been revealed publicly, but on the appointed day it will be revealed for all to see.

Psalm 110 is the psalm which announced 'Operation Footstool', and it is the one quoted in Hebrews. In it God the Father addresses God the Son and says, 'Sit at my right hand until I make your enemies a footstool for your feet' (v1). Some have taken this to mean that Jesus himself will do no more of the work, but will simply wait for the Father to finish it and then receive the kingdom complete. Others take it a step further and say that the Father will use the Church to completely Christianise the world and establish the kingdom. Not only is that a misunderstanding of the Hebrew thinking behind this passage, but it contradicts many other passages in Scripture as well. For example, a few verses further down, in verse 5, God the Son who is 'The Lord . . . at your right hand' is said to be the one who will 'crush kings on the day of his wrath', and it continues in verse 6, 'He will judge nations, heaping up the dead and crushing the rulers of the whole earth'. Far from sitting and waiting, Jesus is said to be the one who goes out in victorious conquest.

'The end will come, when he (Jesus) hands over the kingdom to God the Father after he (Jesus) has destroyed all dominion, authority and power' (1 Cor. 15.24). Furthermore, the description in Revelation 19 and 20 is of the Lord Jesus himself coming as a Mighty Conqueror. Jesus will 'remain in heaven until the time comes for God to restore everything, as he promised long ago through his holy prophets' (Acts 3.21), but when that time comes Jesus will return in power, 'to strike down the nations' (Rev. 19.15).

How then are we to understand the words of Psalm 110.1? It becomes obvious when the background is known. Although we know that Jesus was the specific fulfilment of this psalm, it applied to every king of the Jews as well. A king of Israel was seen as one chosen and anointed by God to occupy God's earthly throne. In 1 Chronicles 29.23 it says, 'So Solomon sat on the throne of the Lord as king'. The authority that the king, rulers and judges had was seen as God's authority, and if people opposed them they were seen as opposing God himself.[1]

Psalm 110 was read at the coronation ceremony of every king and it showed that God was fighting for Israel. It certainly wasn't taken as a command for the king to sit impassively by, doing nothing. Indeed, the kings led their troops into battle. But whenever a battle was won the testimony of scripture was that 'the lord delivered them into our hands', or 'delivered us from the hands of our enemy' (see 1 Sam. 7.3; 2 Sam. 22.1–4; 1 Chron. 11.14; Ezra 8.31). They fought but the Lord was the one who gave them the victory over their enemies.[2] This is seen very clearly in the account in Exodus 17.8–13 of the Israelites' battle with the Amalekites. Moses, Aaron and Hur stood on a hill overlooking the battle. When Moses raised his hands the Israelites prevailed, but when he lowered his hands the Amalekites prevailed. It was a reminder to Joshua and the army that, though they were physically doing the fighting, only God could give them the victory. So although God will make the Lord's enemies his footstool, when the time appointed comes, it will be Jesus who will rise up, return to the earth and establish his rule.

For two thousand years Jesus has been in heaven interceding for his church, but the end of this era of grace is approaching. On the Cross, Jesus won the complete victory and dominion, but he has allowed Satan's rule over the earth to continue and has delayed his day of wrath so that as many as possible may be saved. But when 'the full number of the Gentiles has come in . . . The deliverer will come from Zion' (Romans 11.25 and 26).

Many have used the extension of this period of grace to support their claims that the idea of a personal return of Christ is a myth or simplistic nonsense. Peter prophesied that they would: 'In the last days scoffers will come, scoffing and following their evil desires. They will say

"Where is this 'coming' he promised? Ever since our fathers died, everything goes on as it has since the beginning of creation"' (2 Peter 3.3 and 4). But he adds, 'The Lord is not slow in keeping his promise, as some understand slowness. He is patient with you, not wanting anyone to perish, but everyone to come to repentance' (2 Peter 3.9). The day and hour is already set and when Jesus returns he will mobilise 'Operation Footstool'[3] which will continue until the New Heaven and New Earth of Revelation 21 is established.

It will be sufficient for us to trace Operation Footstool in Christ's victory over death. 1 Corinthians 15.26 states that 'the last enemy to be destroyed is death' i.e. when death is fully dealt with everything else will be, too. Just as the effects of Adam's sin became universal, so will the effects of Christ's victory over death. At the very end no one at all will remain in physical death. Those unbelievers who happily go to their deaths expecting oblivion will be very shocked indeed for 'it is appointed unto men once to die, but after this the judgment' (Heb. 9.27 KJV). Daniel declared that 'Multitudes who sleep in the dust of the earth will awake: some to everlasting life, others to shame and everlasting contempt' (Dan. 12.2).

Death must have felt cheated when Enoch and Elijah were translated out of this earthly realm without dying, and perplexed when a few individuals like Lazarus were temporarily raised, but as we have seen in earlier chapters the really devastating blow was the resurrection of Christ. He had entered voluntarily into the realm of death, had remained in it for three days and three nights and had then, as it were, forced back the fingers of death to escape permanently. It was the first complete victory over death. Today death still holds millions of people, but the stages of death's defeat are clear. When Jesus returns for his Church the 'dead *in* Christ' will rise. 'For the Lord himself shall come down from heaven, with a loud command, with the voice of the archangel and with the trumpet call of God, and the dead in Christ will rise first' (1 Thess. 4.16). Millions of living believers who are 'in Christ' will escape the hands of death forever.

Then believers from other periods will rise. They are not members of Christ's body, but include the Old Testament believers. Job hoped for resurrection. He said, 'I know that my Redeemer lives, and that in the end he will stand upon the earth. And after my skin has been destroyed, yet *in my flesh* I will see God; I myself will see him with my own eyes – I, and not another' (Job 19.25 and 26).

At the very end every unbeliever will be raised and will stand before the throne of God. 'And I saw the dead, great and small, standing before the throne, and books were opened' (Rev. 20.12). At that time death will be left empty-handed and totally vanquished. Having been the ultimate enemy of mankind since the fall of Adam when sin entered into the world, and having been a source of fear to millions, the reign of sin and death will be terminated. 'Then death and Hades were thrown into the lake of fire' (v14).

Although we await the manifestation of this release on the earth, Jesus has already won it on the Cross. In heaven he is awaiting the time in his Father's plan when he will return. This time it will not be as a suffering servant, as it was when he first came and was rejected by his own people. This time it will be as the King of all creation, the prince of glory and the captain of the hosts of the Lord.

Our resurrection bodies will be physical bodies which will be like his glorious body. They will be released from their present limitations to be free of every blemish and disease. These things are not spiritual fables but physical reality. Peter says, 'We did not follow cleverly invented stories when we told you about the power and coming of our Lord Jesus Christ, but we were eye-witnesses of his majesty' (2 Peter 1.16), and he is referring to the time on the Mount of Transfiguration when Jesus appeared before Peter, James and John in the glorious resurrection body which he will have at his Second Advent. Paul also, having referred to Jesus as the first-fruits then continues in 1 Corinthians 15 to speak of our future body. 'The body that is sown is perishable, it is raised imperishable; it is sown in dishonour, it is raised in glory; it is sown in weakness, it is raised in power; it is sown a natural body, it is raised a spiritual one' (1 Cor. 15.42–44). 'As we have borne the likeness of the earthly man so shall we bear the likeness of the man from heaven' (v49). 'When the perishable has been clothed with the imperishable, and the mortal with immortality, then the saying that is written will come true. "Death has been swallowed up in victory. Where, O death, is your victory? Where, O death, is your sting?" . . . Thanks be to God! He gives us the victory through our Lord Jesus Christ' (v54, 55 and 57).

The Bible gives several indications of the nature of our resurrection bodies. These are some of the characteristics[4] they will have:-

1. They will be 'spiritual' bodies (1 Cor. 15.44–46).
2. They will be independent of external constraints and will be able to appear wherever we desire – Jesus appeared to the disciples in a closed room (John 20.19).
3. They will not be subject to tiredness, sickness, hunger or thirst, and while eating will be possible, it won't be necessary (Luke 24.42 and 43).
4. They will be free of mourning, crying and pain and will be filled with bliss (Rev. 21.4).
5. They will be radiant, like the body of Jesus (Matt. 17.1 and 2).
6. Most wonderful of all, they will be conformed to the likeness of Jesus himself (1 John 3.2).

This is our glorious hope. Because Jesus died, rose and ascended as a man in a human body, he has provided a physical victory as well as a spiritual one. Operation Footstool releases us into his total victory, and while we may see some manifestations of it in our present lives, all of this will be overshadowed by the glorious unveiling which will happen at his appearing. Like Job we know that even in our flesh we shall see God.

'And we eagerly await a Saviour from there (heaven), the Lord Jesus Christ, who, by the power that enables him to bring everything under his control, will transform our lowly bodies so that they will be like his glorious body' (Phil. 3.20 and 21).

When Jesus returns he will also destroy Satan and all of his demons. While totally disarmed at the Cross, they have still been active and in stages their activity will be stopped. When Jesus first appears Satan is not thrown into the lake of fire, but is locked away. 'And I saw an angel coming down out of heaven, having the key to the Abyss and holding in his hand a great chain. He seized the dragon, that ancient serpent, who is the devil, or Satan, and bound him for a thousand years. He threw him into the Abyss, and locked and sealed it over him, to keep him from deceiving the nations any more until the thousand years were ended' (Rev. 20.1–3).

The details of the thousand years are beyond the scope of this book, but at the end of them the final stage of Satan's defeat is enacted.

'When the thousand years are over, Satan will be released from his prison and will go out to deceive the nations in the four corners of the earth – Gog and Magog – to gather them for battle (v7). The people who have occupied the earth during this one thousand year period have to be tested in respect of their loyalty to God. By the release of Satan the choice will be given to them. With the final revolt under way, God will directly intervene and, in the book of Revelation, John describes the scene: 'fire came from heaven and devoured them' (Rev. 20.9).

'And the devil, who deceived them, was thrown into the lake of burning sulphur' (Rev. 20.10).

At the very end everything is gathered under the Lordship of Jesus, and the outright victory he won on the Cross is revealed for all eternity. The devil and his angels are in the lake of fire together with the unbelievers who are the 'seed' or 'offspring' of the devil (Gen. 3.15); death and hell are also there, and the fall of man is completely reversed.

The completion of Operation Footstool is in the establishment of the new heaven and the new earth. With the lake of fire burning forever as a testimony to God's absolute righteousness and justice, the new heaven and new earth reflect his love and glory and forever proclaim the victory of Jesus. That there is no further fall is beautifully expressed in the little, often overlooked phrase 'and there was no longer any sea'. The sea, which occupies seventy per cent of the earth's surface today, was part of God's provision in grace. Without it, poisonous waste products and disease, which have resulted from the fall, would have destroyed all life. God designed it as a kind of antiseptic, making it salty to kill the bacteria and to stop putrefaction. He also made it to be the earth's major source of life-giving oxygen. On the new earth there will be no need for a sea because the fall will be gone and there will be no pollution. Then the truth which believers preach today will be seen – that to know God and to let him rule in our lives is perfect peace, perfect happiness and perfect fulfilment. 'Now the dwelling of God is with men, and he will live with them. They will be his people, and God himself will be their God. He will wipe every tear from their eyes. There will be no more death or mourning or crying or pain, for the old order of things has passed away' (Rev. 21.3 and 4).

There is nothing in the universe which can stop his plan – he is sovereign. Jesus Christ is the King of

Kings and Lord of Lords, and God gives us the victory in him.

He is coming soon. 'Amen. Come, Lord Jesus' (Rev. 22.20).

12: The conclusion of the matter

Paul's prayer in Ephesians 1.17–19 was 'that the God of our Lord Jesus Christ, the glorious Father, may give you the Spirit of wisdom and revelation, so that you may know him better. I pray also that the eyes of your heart may be enlightened in order that you may know the hope to which he has called you, the riches of his glorious inheritance in the saints, and his incomparably great power for us who believe'. It is the Holy Spirit who is answering Paul's prayer in our day and more and more believers are being liberated by the truth. The work of our beloved Lord and Saviour Jesus Christ on the Cross has been made ours by the ministry of the Holy Spirit, who baptised us into the body of Christ. At the same time our status before God has been dramatically changed. We who were alienated from God, in slavery to sin because of the fall, and under Satan's dominance have been 'brought nigh', released and made more than conquerors.

It was a deliberate decision by the Lord to call his new people the Church, for the Greek word for church, *ekklesia*, means the 'called out ones'. It was the word used by the Greeks for a meeting of a city council whose members came from ordinary walks of life. They were called out from their normal pursuits to meet together. We have been called out of all we inherited through our natural birth. We have been called out of Adam and put into Christ; out of our racial background (i.e. Jew or Gentile) and made one new man; called out of death and into life; out of judgment and into peace with God; out of the world and into heaven; and out 'from the power of darkness' into 'the kingdom of his dear Son' (Col. 1.13 KJV). Indeed God's purpose is 'to take out . . . a people for his name' (Acts 15.14 KJV). We are the company of the redeemed, the royal family and priesthood of God. 'But you are a chosen people, a royal priesthood, a holy nation, a people belonging to God, that you may declare the praises of him who called you out of darkness into his wonderful light. Once you were not a people, but now you are the people of God; once you had not received mercy, but now you have received mercy' (1 Peter 2.9 and 10).

In the Greek cities no one could vote or join in the discussion of the ekklesia, unless they fulfilled three conditions: 1. They had to be citizens of the city and live within its borders; 2. They had to be free men; 3. They had to be guiltless before the law. These conditions apply equally to us.[1]

1. *Citizenship*

To be a citizen of a city you had to be born there and be living there permanently. We qualify on both counts for when we were born again we were born from above and are now 'seated . . . with him in the heavenly realms in Christ Jesus' (Eph. 2.6), dwelling there permanently. We are under heaven's rules and authority. Our king is there and our thoughts and longings are there. Hence we are entitled to claim all the benefits and protection of heaven. Philippians 3.20 says, 'Our citizenship is in heaven. And we eagerly await a Saviour from there'. Jesus said, 'My prayer is not that you take them out of the world but that you protect them from the evil one. They are not of the world, even as I am not of it' (John 17.15 and 16). We may dwell in this world, but we are of heaven. God's will for us is that in the short time we remain on the earth we should act as ambassadors, showing forth all the glories of our king. He wants us to shine as lights in the world, living lives of victory and holiness and walking in this world as if we were walking the very streets of heaven.

2. *Free-men.*

We were born in bondage, but born again into freedom. We were 'slaves to sin' but he has redeemed us and set us free. 'So you are no longer a slave, but a son; and since you are a son, God has made you also an heir' (Gal. 4.7). 'You, my brothers, were called to be free' (Gal. 5.13). Neither are we in bondage to the devil for John tells us of the believer that Jesus 'who was born of God keeps him safe, and the evil one does not touch him' (1 John 5.18).

3. *Guiltless.*

No criminal was ever allowed to be part of the ekklesia. We were born sinners and were guilty of sin and so in the natural realm we would be excluded. But through the work of Christ we have been justified. 'Righteousness from God comes through faith in Jesus Christ to all who believe' (Romans 3.22).

In every way, therefore, through the work of Christ we are qualified to be the Church of the living God.

We are not here to be dominated by the world and the devil, but rather to exercise God's power over them. To the angels we have a very specific ministry. Ephesians 3.10 tells us what it is: 'His intent was that now, *through the church*, the manifold wisdom of God should be made known to the rulers and authorities in the heavenly realms, according to his eternal purpose which he accomplished in Christ Jesus our Lord' (author's emphasis). It is through the church that the angels are learning things about God's wisdom. 1 Peter 1.12 tells us that 'even angels long to look into these things'. Demons learn about the completeness of the work of Christ and probably know better than us the totality of their defeat.

'Do you not know that we will judge angels?' Paul said to the believers in Corinth (1 Cor. 6.3). Such is our authority in Christ.

Our presence also speaks to the world. 'But thanks be to God, who always leads us in triumphal procession in

Christ and through us spreads everywhere the fragrance of the knowledge of him' (2 Cor. 2.14). Paul again uses the picture of the triumphal Roman procession during which the prisoners of war would be paraded through the streets. We who were formerly God's enemies have been overcome and captured by him, and are led and displayed by him to the world every day and in every place. We are his trophies.

Paul takes the analogy still further. He refers to the custom of burning spices as the procession passed through the streets, in order to fill the city with sweet odours. So Paul continues 'For we are to God the aroma of Christ among those who are being saved and those who are perishing. To the one we are the smell of death; to the other, the fragrance of life' (2 Cor. 2.15 and 16). It is important to note that our aroma is not of ourselves but 'of Christ'. Our bodies are but the vessels in which Christ dwells. Just as Simon said that Jesus would be 'destined to cause the falling and rising of many in Israel and to be a sign that will be spoken against' (Luke 2.34), so therefore are we. As Calvin said of the Gospel we preach by our words and life 'it is never preached in vain, but is effectual leading either to life or death.'

To unbelievers we are an appalling odour of death because we shatter the illusions of their self-imposed blinkered existence. We talk about sin, accountability, judgment and death – all things they would rather forget – and our lives show we are not of this world. We are told 'do not love the world or anything in the world. . . . For everything in the world – the cravings of sinful man, the lust of his eyes and the boasting of what he has and does – comes not from the Father but from the world. The world and its desires pass away, but the man who does the will of God lives forever' (1 John 2.15–17). So to the world we are 'the smell of death'. To other believers or to those who desire the truth however, we are the fragrance of life. I remember very well the peace, love and joy in a fellow student's eyes which first preached the Gospel to me.

In our prayers we are also used. God often achieves his will on this earth by the prayers of the saints. We have already seen that at the end of Ephesians 6, after Paul has listed the armour we need he adds, 'And pray in the Spirit on all occasions with all kinds of prayers and requests' (v18). Effective prayer occurs in the power of the Holy Spirit, for it is he who reveals God's will to us so that we can pray about it. 'If we ask anything according to his will, he hears us. And if we know that he hears us – whatever we ask – we know that we have what we asked of him' (1 John 5.14 and 15).

This way we can intervene directly in the affairs of the world and can thwart Satan's plans. God said to Jeremiah, 'See, today I appoint you over nations and kingdoms to uproot and tear down, to destroy and overthrow, to build and to plant' (Jer. 1.10). This has become the ministry available to us through prayer. Because of our new status in Christ we are heavenly, spiritual people who are now of higher rank than the evil powers of darkness. Therefore, we are able to overthrow them. Praying specifically for our towns and cities, our regions and our country is part of our task, and thereby we can achieve great successes. Anything which opposes God can and should be opposed by us in our prayers. We can pray against terrorism, for peace, for the removal of the cults and sex shops, and we can intercede on behalf of our nation, our royal family, our government and our land. Like Moses we need to stand on the hill top while the battle rages and lift our hands to God.

Not only has Christ's work delivered us from the pollution and decay of this world, but it is so effective that it has made us the salt of the earth. We are an instrument of God's grace to this earth, because our presence commands God's blessing and our prayers ensure that the headlong rush of evil does not continue unopposed.

For ourselves, however, let us shake off the shackles. Jesus read from the scroll of Isaiah and said, 'The Spirit of the Lord is on me, because he has anointed me to preach good news to the poor. He has sent me to proclaim freedom for the prisoners and recovery of sight for the blind, to release the oppressed, to proclaim the year of the Lord's favour'. And then while all eyes were upon him he added, 'Today this scripture is fulfilled in your hearing' (Luke 4.18, 19 and 21). That era of favour is still open and all who have received Christ as their Saviour can claim the fulness of his work. If while we were unsaved and enemies of Christ, God did the utmost for us by sending his Son to die for us, will he do any less now that we are his sons and daughters? Of course not. Our problem is that we do not possess our inheritance. When God promised that 'every valley shall be raised up, every mountain and hill made low' (Isaiah 40.4), it was not just a geographical promise but one for each one of us to claim in our lives. The valleys of despair and defeat are turned by Jesus Christ into sunny mountain tops, with those who have lacked love becoming the most loving; those who were depressed, overflowing with joy and those who were most oppressed soaring as free as eagles. He has won our freedom and given to us his overwhelming victory – the devil *is* under our feet.

Let us rise as the church triumphant and march forward in all that he has provided for us. The commandment of the Spirit of God so long ago to the Jews is urgently exhorting us today:-

'Awake, awake, O Zion, clothe yourself with strength.
Put on your garments of splendour, O Jerusalem, the holy city.
Shake off your dust; rise up, sit enthroned, O Jerusalem.
Free yourself from the chains on your neck,
O captive daughter of Zion' (Isaiah 52.1 and 2).

Notes

Chapter One.

1. See:
   Os Guinness 'The Dust of Death' IVP 1973.
   Francis Schaeffer 'The God Who is There' Pickering & Inglis 1982.

Further reading on this topic:-
   Merrill F. Unger: 'Demons in the World Today'. Tyndale House Publishers 1971.
   Hal Lindsey: 'Satan is Alive & Well on Planet Earth'. Lakeland 1973.

Chapter Two.

1. 'The Screwtape Letters'. C. S. Lewis. Collins Fontana Books. 1973. p. 9.
2. I am grateful to Arthur C. Custance for the basic ideas behind this section – see 'The Fall was Down'. A. C. Custance. Doorway Paper No. 40. 1967.
3. M. B. Eddy 'Science and Health with Key to the Scriptures' (Boston, First Church of Christ, Scientist). p. 243–4
4. Jacques Monod 'Chance and Necessity'. trans. A. Wainhouse (N.Y. Alfred A. Knopf 1971) pp. 155f.
5. Samuel Limbach as quoted by E. Sauer, in 'The King of the Earth'. The Paternoster Press 1962. p. 74.
6. Eric Sauer 'The Dawn of World Redemption'. Eerdmans, Grand Rapids 1953 p. 61.
7. For example: M. R. De Haan 'Religion or Christ'. Radio Bible Class P. O. Box 22, Grand Rapids, Michigan p. 17–23.
8. R. D. G. Price 'In the Beginning' Dunestone Press, Newton Abbott, Devon. 1978.
9. I am grateful to Prof. Bruce K. Waltke of Dallas Theological Seminary for the background thoughts.

See also Charles Clough 'A Framework for Christian Doctrine' Section 2 and 3. Lubbock Bible Church, Lubbock, Texas 79410.

Chapter Three.

1. While it is beyond the scope of this book it is interesting to note that the word 'desire' is the Hebrew word *tshuka* which comes from an Arabic root meaning 'to seek control' as it is used in Gen. 4.7b. Hence its fuller meaning might be that the woman seeks to control her husband. The author tends to this view.
2. Chrysostom as quoted by H.C. Leupold in 'Exposition of Genesis' Vol. One. The Wartbug Press 1980. p. 163.
3. M. R. De Haan 'Religion or Christ', Radio Bible Class. P.O. Box 22, Grand Rapids, Michigan p. 17–23.

Chapter Four.

1. The classic book on the Virgin Birth is 'The Virgin Birth of Christ' by J. Gresham Machen. Baker Book House, Grand Rapids, Michigan. 1977.
2. I am grateful to L. S. Chafer for many of these ideas. See L. S. Chafer 'Systematic Theology. Dallas Seminary Press 1947. Vol. 5.
3. Shelley W. B. and H. J. Hurley "Methods of Exploring Human Apocrine Sweat Gland Physiology", Arch. Dermat. and Syph. 66 1952 pp. 156–161.
4. Maldonatus Joannes 'Commentary on the Four Gospels'. Paris 1639. p. 601.
5. de Mezaray 'Histoire de France'. Paris 1685 Vol. 3 p. 306.
6. See A. C. Custance 'How did Jesus die'. Doorway Paper No. 17.
7. As quoted in Bishop Christopher Wordsworth 'Commentary on the Gospel of St. Matthew'. Rivingtons, London 1870.

A. C. Custance 'The Seed of the Woman'. Doorway Publications has been an invaluable source.

Chapter Five.

Several books have been helpful in this chapter and in chapter 6.

H. Brash Bonsall. 'The Person of Christ'. CLC 1967.
T. C. Hammond. 'In Understanding be Men'. IVP 1965.
L. S. Chafer. 'Major Bible Themes'. Zondervan 1974.
Eric Sauer. 'The Triumph of the Crucified' Paternoster Press 1953.

Chapter Six.

1. N. B. Petra is feminine in the greek and must, therefore, apply to a feminine noun. The word 'homologia' which means 'confession' and is also feminine and this led the earliest writers to the conclusion that it was Peter's confession of him as Christ to which Jesus was referring. All of them disclaim any idea of its' referring to Peter himself, but instead emphasise HIM who was the subject of Peter's confession.

Chapter Seven.

1. Quoted by H. Brash Bonsall in his book 'The Person of Christ' C. L. C. 1967 p. 152.
2. For more detail see F. Delitzsch's commentary on the Psalms. Eerdmans reprint 1978. pp. 152–154
3. See B. F. Westcott 'The Epistle to the Hebrews'. Macmillan 1889 p. 44.

Chapter Eight.

1. See J. F. Walvoord's 'The Revelation of Jesus Christ'. Marshall, Morgan & Scott. 1966. p. 59.

Chapter Nine.

1. See Peter Connolly 'The Roman Army' Macdonald Educational 1976. p. 74.

Chapter Ten.

1. Cambridge Ancient History. Volume IX; p. 374.
2. K. S. Wuest 'Golden Nuggets' Eerdmans. 1973. p. 102.

Chapter Eleven.

1. This was still recognised by the English monarchy as late as 1660. On Saturday June 23rd 1660 King Charles 2nd held an annual ceremony of healing when 600 people touched him to be cured of their diseases. It was held at the Banqueting Hall.
2. For an excellent discussion of this see F. Delitzsch 'Psalms'. Eerdmans Reprint 1978. p. 183–196.
3. I am grateful to R. B. Thieme Jnr. for this title.
4. For more details see E. Sauer 'The Triumph of the Crucified'. The Paternoster Press 1953. p. 123ff.

Chapter Twelve.

1. E. Sauer 'The Triumph of the Crucified'. The Paternoster Press 1953 p. 61.
2. As quoted by Philip E. Hughes in 'The Second Epistle to the Corinthians' Eerdmans 1977 p. 81.